I Wanna

Be Sedated

Sound And Vision
Toronto

I Wanna Be Sedated

Be Sedated

Pop Music in the Seventies

Phil Dellio & Scott Woods

Sound And Vision
Toronto

Contents

Acknowledgements

Phil Dellio — For reasons that may or may not seem mysterious to them, thanks goes out to the following people: Angela Barker, Edith Bartlett, Chris Buck, Chris Cook, Frank Kogan, Dave MacIntosh, Pam Martin, Dave Porter, Mike Saunders, Rob Sheffield, Peter Stephens, and Jack Thompson. Most of all I owe gratitude to the guy who co-wrote *I Wanna Be Sedated,* and also to Chuck Eddy — if I listed the things I should be thanking Chuck for, suggesting Scott and me for this book would rank about seventh.

Scott Woods — I thank Jason Armstrong, Dave Bookman, Chris Buck, Chuck Eddy, Kelvin Holland, Dave Newfeld, Sean O'Connor, and Tom Sawyer, all of whom helped in various ways. Thanks also to everyone in my family for their support, especially Grandma Linton. Finally, I'm forever grateful to Phil Dellio, who never failed to make me laugh, and my brother Paul for introducing me to *Slayed?* at a very young age.

Both of us would like to thank Geoff Savage, Jacky Savage, and Jonathan Savage of Sound And Vision for helping us every step of the way; also, Dave Prothero for his illustrations and for thinking up the title. We used a number of sources in researching quotes, dates, and biographical information, the most helpful of which were *The Rolling Stone Illustrated History of Rock & Roll, 2nd edition* (ed. Jim Miller), *The Rolling Stone Encyclopedia of Rock & Roll* (eds. Jon Pareles and Patricia Romanowski), Irwin Stambler's *Encyclopedia of Pop, Rock & Soul,* Nick Logan's and Bob Woffinden's *Illustrated Encyclopedia of Rock,* Fred Bronson's *The Billboard Book of Number-One Hits, Stranded* (ed. Greil Marcus), old issues of *Creem* and *Rolling Stone,* and especially Joel Whitburn's desert-island *Top Pop Singles 1955 - 1986,* which is the one place to go if you want to try to piece together the world of Daddy Dewdrop, Claudja Barry, and Andrew Gold.

Dedication

For our parents

Peter and Patricia Dellio   Stuart and Eileen Woods

WE HAD JOY, WE HAD FUN

It's instructive to think back to the summer of 1973 for a moment, a time when Billy Preston made it to the top of North American record charts by asking a question that has since haunted every adolescent who grew up in the seventies: "Will it go round in circles?" The answer, which should be clear to anyone witnessing the current boom in bell bottoms, disco nostalgia, and CBs (which, oddly enough, people now insist on calling CDs), is a resounding Yes. As to the meaning of this improbable seventies revival, once again you can't do better than to quote from Billy's follow-up hit, "Nothing from Nothing"— it leaves nothing, he concluded, and we agree. So don't expect any grand theorizing in these pages on the Golden Earring iconography in the third Soundgarden album, or the deep-seated epistemological bond between Van McCoy and the Red Hot Chili Peppers. If we stumble onto even a fraction of Billy's philosophical insight, we'll accomplish more than we set out to do.

What we've written instead is an informal survey of pop music in the 1970s, by which we mean everything that reached us and probably you during those years, especially if you were situated anywhere near a radio — everything from ABBA to Zeppelin, and much, much more in between. It was a decade that saw the proliferation of dozens of genres, subgenres, and demigenres, with each one frantically trying to outdo the other in hype, gluttony, fads, decibels, and perfectly silly records. At the end of it all, pop music emerged from the seventies as a radically transformed creature from the one that stepped into the decade — clearly there's a world of difference between B.J. Thomas, who had the first number-one single of the seventies, and Rupert Holmes, who had the last — and that's the story we're after.

With so much going on, it would take an encyclopedia to catalogue every last performer who contributed to this evolution, but this is not that encyclopedia. *I Wanna Be Sedated* chooses from amongst a morass of names, and focuses only on those that best reflect the spirit of the 1970s that we're most interested in capturing. One kind of artist who gets shortchanged along the way — sometimes even left out altogether — is the sixties legend who made some fine (and many not-so-fine) records in the seventies but didn't have a lot to do with the decade that we're writing about, the one celebrated by *Wayne's World*, *The Simpsons*, *Reservoir Dogs*, and Rhino Records' *Have a Nice Day* series. This happened to Bob Dylan, Van Morrison, Aretha Franklin, and Tom Jones. Another way to miss the cut was to make music that could not logically be plunked into any of the chapters we've set up. Hybrid artists like Traffic, Dire Straits, 10cc, and Spirit were too difficult to slot, so we skipped them altogether — anyone who sufficiently confused us was given their walking papers. We made an ethical decision to stay clear of anyone whose name could be construed as containing a drug allusion, so there's nothing about the Poppy Family. Finally, our original plan was to exclude everyone whose music we'd never heard, but in the end we decided that wouldn't be fair. We won't name names, though.

Because *I Wanna Be Sedated* is not intended as a book of rock criticism, emphasis is not always placed where others would have it. Stevie Wonder and Neil Young, who many consider the decade's two most significant artists, are dealt with relatively briefly. On the other hand, Cheap Trick, ABBA, and Kiss get chapters to themselves. Richard and Linda Thompson, Gram Parsons, and John Cale are nowhere to be found because we had to make room for Mocedades, A Taste of Honey, and Rex Smith instead. At the margins, there is a geographical bias that favors American artists over British artists (and an even stronger one that favors British artists over Latvian artists). We tried to correct this by writing the original manuscript in Chaucerian English, but it just didn't work.

It's best to think of *I Wanna Be Sedated* as our version of that greatest of all seventies inventions, the 8-Track tape. Just as with any 8-Track, it's a book that's handy to carry around. Every effort has been made to encompass artists in the space of a single chapter, but sometimes we had to split someone over two chapters — it wouldn't be like a real 8-Track if there weren't annoying edits. You'll want to take great care not to leave your copy out in the sun too long, else it might warp, melt, and start to sound funny. And best of all, someday — maybe five years from now, maybe ten years from now — you're going to be able to buy this book for 99¢.

Chapter 1

DENNY LAINE IS IN MY EARS AND IN MY EYES

Howard: "It's a joy to have you with us, John."
John: "Thank you, Howard. It's a pleasure to be here
and it's great to meet you after seeing you on TV so much."
Howard: "It's a treasured moment for you, isn't it?"
John: "It is — it's one of the highlights."
— *Howard Cosell and John Lennon*, 1974.

THE 1970s did not begin overnight. (Actually they did, but this is a music book, not a science text.) The seventies was disco and punk, K-Tel and heavy metal, Don Kirshner and CB radios, double-live albums and the Knack. But on January 1, 1970, the only one of them that was much of a story was heavy metal, which had just taken a huge leap in visibility a mere five weeks earlier with the release of Led Zeppelin's "Whole Lotta Love," a staggering portent of the decade ahead. We'll get to those seventies, the real seventies, later.

Meanwhile, the seventies began exactly as you might expect: the fabled 1960s decided to hang around a little longer, sometimes drifting along for another three or four years, sometimes sticking it out for the whole of the next decade, and in rare cases thriving right through until the 1990s, at which time the sixties began masquerading under strange nicknames like 'Lenny Kravitz,' 'Wilson Phillips,' and 'the Grateful Dead.' Depending upon how you felt about the sixties in the first place, this extended stay was either like a good friend coming to visit and then agreeing to stick around for a few extra days, or a deadbeat tenant who just wouldn't clear the premises. In either case, any book on pop music in the 1970s has to begin with an itinerary of how the sixties' major hangers-on fared throughout the decade. And certainly no one was more major in the sixties, or did more hanging on in the seventies, than the Beatles.

The story of the Beatles in the 1970s, both collectively and individually, had everything and nothing to do with the new decade. It had everything to do with the seventies because, following the Beatles' breakup in 1970, the trajectory of their subsequent solo work established a pattern followed by many of their sixties peers: after a brief flash of promise, it was mostly just a long and winding house of mirrors for the four Beatles, and the same was more or less true of Bob Dylan, the Who, the Beach Boys, the Turtles, Bobby Goldsboro, and many others. You could, if you wanted to, say the end of the Beatles created a vacuum from which more than a few careers never recovered.[1] At the same time, however, the Beatles had *nothing* to do with the 1970s, because once out on their own they remained doggedly oblivious to all that surrounded them. It's actually possible to document the comings and goings of the four ex-Beatles in the seventies without once having to mention glam, *Dance Fever*, CBGBs, or Britt Ekland. That in itself was an accomplishment, sort of.

"All you need are vermin-like lawyers!" was the Beatles' rallying cry in the first few months of the decade as they kept busy by sniping at each other in public, sneaking off behind each other's backs to work on solo projects, trying to keep their failing Apple Corporation afloat, and fighting for control of their own song catalogue (the biggest issue being who'd get stuck with "Revolution #9"). But they hadn't shut down operations yet; they were still the Beatles and they were still charting records. *Abbey Road* (released in late 1969) battled with *Led Zeppelin II* for the number one spot on both sides of the Atlantic, *Hey Jude* (1970) successfully recycled some old singles for the American market, and *Let It Be*'s title track (1970) landed smack in the middle

---

[1] Which would also explain the death of J. Edgar Hoover in 1972 and the break-up of heavy metal band Dust in 1973, two other tragedies that were clearly vacuum-related.

of a stirring number-one gospel trilogy that included Simon & Garfunkel's "Bridge Over Troubled Water" and Ray Stevens' "Everything Is Beautiful"; all signs were pointing to a big decade ahead for Tennessee Ernie Ford. With *Let It Be* as the Beatles' ragtag exit, we'll turn away from the legal entanglements left behind by their official dissolution in the spring of 1970 and focus attention on their post-Beatles solo work.

Without doubt it was John Lennon, always the most mercurial and cerebral of the Beatles (well, OK, Ringo was more versed in French theater and differential calculus), who experienced the loftiest peaks and lowest valleys. He began the decade in great shape: an excellent single ("Instant Karma," 1970), two acclaimed and adventurous albums (*Plastic Ono Band*, 1970, and *Imagine,* 1971), and the companionship of his all-purpose wife Yoko, who doubled as a burglar alarm, smoke detector, and high-decibel dog whistle. *POB* and *Imagine* broke important ground in the confessional singer-songwriter field soon to sweep the pop world as John began exploring a new kind of rhyme structure called 'primal scream'. You can try it yourself by screaming once and then screaming again. See? It rhymes! The albums delved into every corner and crevice of John's embattled psyche by laying bare his relationship to God, his dead mother, his public celebrity, his childhood, and even his ex-songwriting partner Paul McCartney, whom he attacked mercilessly on *Imagine* 's "How Do You Sleep?" (An incensed Paul came back with a sharp rejoinder in *Rolling Stone* 's "McCartney Dismembers" interview: "With three pillows, two pacifiers, and me knees tucked close to me chin—and it's no business of yours, John Lennon!")

But after *Imagine* came a lull that lasted about nine years. *Some Time in New York City* (1972) drove 187 people in a remote Ukrainian fishing village insane, and though *Mind Games* (1973) and *Walls and Bridges* (1974) signaled a return to accessibility, Ringo made better pop music now, and so did the guy who sang "Kung Fu Fighting." John's only other LP in the seventies was *Rock and Roll* (1975) — a collection of covers originally made famous by Flash Cadillac and the Continental Kids — after which he became a non-recording househusband, immersed in a battle with the U.S. government to have the Surgeon General's warning removed from all copies of *Some Time in New York City*. And as any Beatles fan already knows, much better and much worse days lay ahead for John in the eighties.

Whatever John's shortcomings were in the 1970s, at least his idiosyncrasies indicated a pulse. Strictly speaking, Paul McCartney had one too, but who among us didn't wonder if maybe it was true after all, that Paul *was* at least a little bit dead? It wasn't that he was hard to find, in fact he and Wings had more hit singles during the decade than anyone except Elton John, including fifteen in the Top Ten and six number-ones. But from "Another Day" (1971) right through to "Goodnight Tonight" (1979), Paul's output was an almost undisturbed calm of whimsy, preciousness, and chirpy-chirpy-cheep-cheep. His ballads weren't as pretty as the Carpenters', his rock and roll was tamer than the Osmonds', and he didn't have as fundamental a grasp of modern recording technology as C.W. McCall. On the plus side, "Maybe I'm Amazed" (1970) and "Jet" (1974) were as good as all but the best of Paul's Beatles songs, and the rest of his solo work was marked by an engaging self-deprecation (most evident on 1976's "Silly Love Songs") that helped a little. But if Charles Manson were to title his autobiography *Nutty Mass Murderer*, we wouldn't necessarily forgive him, would we?

Unlike John, Paul's post-Beatles career was not documented on his albums; rather, he was a Top Forty automaton, a three-minute warlord in an LP combat zone, a human jukebox run amok. For starters, there were those silly-putty love songs, the archetype being "My Love" from 1973. At the rock end of the spectrum, "Hi Hi Hi" (1972) and "Helen Wheels" (1973) were but two of Paul's unique offerings to the gods of heavy metal thunder. Commandeering the great expanse in between was Paul the Pillsbury Dough Boy on "Uncle Albert/Admiral Halsey" (1971), "Let 'Em In" (1976), and "With a Little Luck" (1978), the first and second of which featured extended kazoo solos — a real breakthrough for rock and roll. Although Paul mostly stayed clear of strident rhetoric, he did find time to address Britain's fractious political climate via stirring endorsements of the Irish ("Give Ireland Back to the Irish," 1972), the Scottish ("Mull of Kintyre," 1977), and the nation's beleaguered sheep farming community ("Mary Had a Little Lamb," 1972). Controversy was John's department, though; outside of an ugly 1978 incident where Paul and his wife Linda were spotted making a third trip to a salad bar with a two-trip limit, the McCartneys' private lives weren't exactly a hotbed of tabloid intrigue.

The paths taken by Paul and John in the 1970s were exactly what any Beatles fan could have expected. The same eventually turned out to be true of George Harrison and Ringo Starr, but shortly after the Beatles' breakup, it was still the case that both were blank slates waiting to be filled in. As it happened, George spent the seventies in a state of suspended animation: partly within himself, partly without himself, but mostly just trying to remember if he left his car keys at the Maharishi's. Initially, George made as much post-Beatles noise as anyone. *All Things Must Pass* (1970) contained a two-sided number-one single in "My Sweet Lord"/"Isn't It a Pity," and *Rolling Stone* called the six-sided set an "extravaganza of piety and sacrifice and joy, whose sheer magnitude and ambition may dub it the *War and Peace* of rock and roll". Which, if nothing else, is better than being the Warren Beatty of rock and roll.

Buoyed by his new-found status as a mystic, philosopher, and Russian novelist of major import, George's next project was the organization of an all-star concert featuring Ringo, Bob Dylan, Leon Russell, Leon Redbone, Redbone, Red Skelton, and others to aid the famine-stricken country of Bangladesh. George's initiative was beyond reproach, but *Concert for Bangla Desh* (1971) did have a few glitches — Ravi Shankar got a whole side to himself, and Billy Preston's hair took up another. Even more questionable were *Living in the Material World* (1973), *Dark Horse* (1974), and *Extra Texture* (1975), while *Thirty-three & 1/3* (1976) went the McCartney route on such preschool sing-songs as "Crackerbox Palace" and "This Song" (which should never ever be confused with that song). George did come back strong in the early eighties with "Metaphysical," his biggest hit ever: "Let's get metaphysical/I wanna get metaphysical/Let me hear your karma talk!"

Because Ringo was the Beatle who aimed lowest in the 1970s, he didn't make out too badly. In fact, included among Ringo's first few releases were probably the two best post-Beatles singles of all, "It Don't Come Easy" (1971) and "Photograph" (1973). The latter appeared on the popular *Ringo* LP, a much-hyped assemblage of all four Beatles on the same album. How did Ringo manage such a coup? Easy. He separately cut some tracks with each for an LP to be called *The Two Guys Who Did Most of the Work in the Beatles*, and then patched it all together through round-the-clock editing. It was just like old times.

Ringo was on a veritable rampage from 1971 to 1975 with "You're Sixteen" (1973), "Oh My My" (1974), "Only You" (1974), and "No No Song" (1975), waging war with Tony Orlando and Bobby Vinton right on their own turf. If Paul was self-deprecating, Ringo was practically apologetic for coming across like the punch-line to "When I'm Sixty Four". As such, he was still the most endearing of the four ex-Beatles, and though his record sales plummeted in the second half of the decade, he did manage to resume his acting career when he landed a starring role opposite Mae West in *Sextette* (1978). He continued in a palaeontological vein for 1981's *Caveman* .

Meanwhile, something remarkable had happened in 1976: a Beatles revival took place in the U.S. and Britain, moving some old singles back onto the charts and squaring off the Beatles of yesterday against the Bay City Rollers, Donny and Marie Osmond, and Nadia Comaneci for teen-sensation-of-the-year bragging rights. Pressure began to mount for a onetime charitable reunion concert, as reports circulated of a multi-million dollar offer from the United Nations, a stunning $3,000 bid from NBC's new *Saturday Night Live* TV show, various other offers dangled by independent promoters, and over-tures made by the International Kiwanis Club, the World Wrestling Federation, and the Girl Guides of America. The four Beatles resisted, though, so in lieu of the real thing, the world settled for *The Rutles* (1978), an inspired Monty Python parody; *Beatlemania* (1976), an inspired stage-show parody; and *Sgt. Pepper's Lonely Hearts Club Band* (1978), part of the popular disaster-film cycle of the 1970s.

There were other diversions, too, in the way of ersatz Beatles for amnesiacs. Britain's Badfinger even received writing and production input from various Beatles, and three of their singles made the Top Ten: "Come and Get It" (1970), "No Matter What" (1970), and "Day After Day" (1971). The band had to pack it in, however, after publicly declaring themselves "more popular than Jesus Alou," a slap in the face to baseball fans everywhere. On the American side, the Raspberries

("Go All the Way," 1972), Big Star, Blue Ash, and Artful Dodger also caused ripples of excitement, but Ed Sullivan was off the air by the time they all got rolling, and a guest shot on *The Mac Davis Show* just didn't carry the same mythic resonance.

The most peculiar Beatles soundalike was Klaatu, a group of mysterious travelers who charted one two-sided single in 1977 ("Sub-Rosa Subway"/"Calling Occupants") and then promptly returned to whence they came. Which, to the surprise of no one except Amazing Kreskin fans, turned out to be a dairy farm in Northern Ontario. Rumors abounded that Klaatu was the Beatles themselves anonymously reunited, which was obviously impossible seeing as John, Paul, George, and Ringo were already anonymously collaborating under the name 'Leo Sayer'.

The Beatles did not have anywhere near the kind of decade that one might have hoped for in the 1970s. Paul made loads of money, and all four Beatles could have contributed some good songs to a one-LP compilation of their solo work. But basically they drifted along without rudder, paddles, or compass, and by the end of the decade the idea of 'Beatle mystique' seemed long gone. If the Beatles lost their way because they consciously chose not to keep up with the seventies, they at least avoided the opposite trap of trying to latch onto every last movement, trend, and blip in the world of pop. Quite content to appreciate "Disco Duck" on its own merits, none of the Beatles felt compelled to get too involved in the issue one way or the other. However, their former number-one rivals tried to match Rick Dees quack-for-quack, and in the process became one of the most entertaining sideshows of the seventies.

Chapter 2

You Probably Think This Chapter's About You

"But when I looked into Mick's eyes, I saw myself a year ago —
a prisoner of the system, playing what the people wanted, not
what they needed. I felt it would be wrong to offend him because
there's a soul inside that body that wants to be free."
— Carlos Santana, 1974.

UNLIKE the Beatles, the Rolling Stones made it through the
seventies intact. It wasn't pretty, though — they trudged where they
once ran, followed where they once led, and groveled abjectly where
they once stood tall. The Stones endured because, unlike their sixties
peers, they jumped on each seventies bandwagon that rumbled by,
squaring off against Elton John, Disco Tex, and the Fabulous Poodles,
and drawing inspiration from them the way they once did from Chuck
Berry and Muddy Waters. Along the way they modestly appointed
themselves 'world's greatest rock and roll band,' laying claim to the
phrase before Three Dog Night, MFSB, and the Ozark Mountain
Daredevils even had a chance.

Building on the momentum of 1969's *Let It Bleed*, the Stones
began the seventies impressively with *Sticky Fingers* (1971) and *Exile
on Main St.* (1972), their best LPs of the decade. *Sticky Fingers* was

highlighted by the ballads "Moonlight Mile" and "Dead Flowers," the eternally indecipherable "Sway," and "Brown Sugar," a nifty dance hit that managed to generate a bit of old-fashioned Stones controversy (protestations came primarily from black Americans, though the dental community was equally outraged). Even during the album's one boring section, the seventy-nine minute jazz-rock coda to "Can't You Hear Me Knocking," listeners were able to amuse themselves by operating the Andy Warhol-designed zipper on the front cover — up and down, up and down...it was fascinating.

On *Exile,* the Stones followed Simon & Garfunkel's lead and went looking for America. The album chronicled a journey that took the group careering down the corridors of various Holiday Inns and Best Western Motels, from New Orleans to Virginia to Las Vegas, stopping en route for Baptist churches, casinos, whorehouses, and roadside honky-tonks. It was in one of the latter, a place called Jimmy Bob Greene's in L.A., that they finally found what they were looking for: hot new band America, rocking some local yokels with a powerhouse rendition of "A Horse With No Name." "I like this," mused Mick Jagger, "I like this very much — let's go looking for Brazil now."

With *Goats Head Soup* (1973) the Stones dove headfirst into the seventies once and for all. It was a scary album — certainly few songs for the remainder of the decade were as horrifying as "Dancing With Mr. D," wherein Mick does the mashed potato and the watusi with Bob Dylan, John Denver, or maybe even Satan himself (nobody's bothered to figure out which). *Soup* also featured "Angie," a number-one ballad inspired by Angela Bowie, Angela Davis, or Angie Dickinson (again, no one's bothered to figure out which, though we do know that it paved the way for Helen Reddy's "Angie Baby"), and "Star Star," a heroic attempt to be more outrageous than Gary Glitter. At the risk of widespread cries of "Waiter, there's a really dumb record in my goats head soup!", let's go out on a limb and predict that seventy-five years from now *Goats Head Soup* will be considered hands-down better than *Jammin' With Edward* (1972), an ad hoc 'jam session' between a few of the Stones and Canada's Edward Bear.

It's Only Rock 'n' Roll (1974) and *Black and Blue* (1976) showed the Stones playing catch-up with everything in sight. The former had nods to glam ("If You Can't Rock Me" and the title track), Caribbean rhythms ("Luxury"), and Pink Floydian introspection ("Time Waits for No One"), while the latter veered off into imitation Ohio Players ("Hot Stuff"), imitation Chi-Lites ("Fool to Cry"), and imitation Harry Belafonte ("Cherry Oh Baby"). *Black and Blue* also marked the debut of guitarist Ron 'Norwegian' Wood into the band, who replaced Mick Taylor and took over as the group's official charcoal sketch artist.

By this time the Stones were being attacked mercilessly by punks who claimed the band was washed up, complacent, decadent, jaded, ridiculous, spineless, pathetic, and tragically ugly besides. "Am not ugly!" yelled Mick. "Are too!" the punks yelled back. Unruffled, the Stones responded with *Some Girls* (1978), the first semi-legitimate best-Stones-disc-since-*Exile* and a record loud, fast, and sloppy enough to send members of Dr. Feelgood and Ducks Deluxe running for cover. "That'll show those pub rockers who's boss," chirped the hard-of-hearing Mick. While *Some Girls* certainly had its share of vintage Stones — Keith Richards' ravaged vocal on "Before They Make Me Run," sex with Margaret Trudeau on "Respectable," the title track's creative recipes for strawberry jam that had the Reverend Jesse Jackson throwing conniptions — it was actually a disco stomp called "Miss You" that took the group back to the top of the charts. "That'll show those Peaches and Herb who's boss," chirped the hard-of-dancing Mick. The album ended with "Shattered," which should have ended the saga altogether: "Shattered, I'm in tatters" would have made for a fitting farewell.

The Stones also had a busy decade outside the recording studio. There was, for instance, Mick's marriage to Bianca Perez Morena de Macias in 1972, the most eagerly anticipated rock and roll wedding since Tiny Tim's marriage to Miss Vicky; the band's infamous social rounds with Truman Capote, Imelda Marcos, Secretariat, and other high-profile celebrities; the spectacle of Mick riding atop a giant inflatable penis on the Stones' 1975 U.S. tour;[1] Bill Wyman's discovery of Tucky Buzzard, a group of Finnish bird watchers he took under his wing as protégés; and Keith's and Ron's 1979 New Barbarians tour, with proceeds going towards the purchase of a new left hand for

[1] Rather redundant seeing as Mick's somewhat of a giant inflatable penis himself.

22

Moulty. Charlie Watts didn't make any news per se, but he did come up with one of the decade's most urbane haircuts for the cover of *Black and Blue.*

The Rolling Stones were virtually a précis of the 1970s, accommodating every shift in public taste and absorbing every trend that passed before their eyes. They absorbed and absorbed and absorbed, until finally they resembled a big wet sponge. With the Beatles on one side of the seventies spectrum (befuddled spectators) and the Stones on the other (avid participants), a big black hole was created in the center, waiting to be filled up by the Who, Bob Dylan, the Cowsills, and other legendary sixties rock stars who had to find their way through the new decade.

Chapter 3

Does Anybody Really Know What Time It Is?

"I recently went to do a BBC-TV interview and when I arrived at the studios there were all these young kids waiting outside for the Bay City Rollers. As I passed them by, one of the kids recognized me and said, 'Ooo look, it's Pete Townshend,' and a couple of them chirped 'Ello Pete.' And that was it."
— Pete Townshend, 1975.

THOUGH none of the remaining sixties artists seemed quite as disinterested in the seventies as the Beatles, some did take the *Plastic Ono* route by issuing brutal 'dream is over' tracts, the most chilling of which was Peter Noone's declaration in *16* magazine that "I don't believe in Herman." Others took a path closer to George Harrison by seeking artistic guidance and long-term career counseling from a spiritual mentor (Meher Baba, Jesus Christ, the Flying Nun). Many stumbled into Rolling Stones territory by discovering roots they never knew they had in disco, reggae, and juju music. A few even followed Stu Sutcliffe and Brian Jones to the sidelines, where they sat back and had a great time watching everyone else thrash about willy-nilly. But the one common thread among Sly Stone, Bob Dylan, Eric Clapton, and other key sixties figures was that they all released an album or two that launched what is now known as the Classic Rock era.

The best place to start is Sly & the Family Stone's *There's a Riot*

24

Goin' On (1971), the big critical favorite of the day and an even harsher rebuttal of cheerier times than the theme song from *All in the Family*. *Riot*'s highlights included a brilliant number-one single, "Family Affair"; "Thank You For Talking To Me Africa," which launched the return-to-the-motherland movement picked up by Thundermug ("Africa"), the Dictators ("Back to Africa"), and Toto ("Africa"); and the title track, a 0:00 work-in-progress that was later turned into a six-second disco extendamix by DJ Venus Flytrap. An immensely popular album, *Riot* sparked one of the most startling periods ever in black pop, but before Sly could fully capitalize on *Riot*'s success, he found himself caught in a bizarre love triangle with Doris Day and Tony Randall that led to some truly erratic behavior on his part: he began to miss concerts, he covered "Que Sera Sera" (1973), and he insisted on vacuuming the Family Stone's tour bus four times a day.

Bob Dylan almost missed the seventies completely, but in 1975 he recovered with *Blood on the Tracks* , an album to rival his best sixties work. On the LP's standout tracks, "Idiot Wind" and "Tangled Up in Blue," Dylan documented the breakup of his marriage in dramatic fashion, a theme he would return to in his 1978 film *Geraldo and Farrah*. The album also launched the Minneapolis sound that would dominate pop music in the mid-eighties; displeased with the LP's original demos, Bob hired local musicians Morris Day, Jimmy Jam, Tommy Stinson, Bob Mould, and the Jets for a bang-up acoustic lollapalooza. *Blood* was Bob's seventies wake-up call: thereafter, he donned Kiss makeup on his 1976 Rolling Thunder Revue tour, followed Cheap Trick to Budokan for a live set in 1979, and then signed off with "Gotta Serve Somebody" (1979), reinventing new wave as it might have sounded just days before the first Dire Straits album.

The Who's Pete Townshend also embarked on a spiritual quest in the seventies, seeking inspiration from his mentor Meher Baba for most of the decade. Meher's presence was especially felt on *Who's Next* (1971), the group's most accomplished album of the seventies, which had rock fans everywhere spontaneously forming circles and chanting "Ba-Ba-Ba, Ba-Ba O'Riley." The album featured a couple of perennial anthems in "Behind Blue Eyes" and "Won't Get Fooled Again," both of which inspired millions of concert-goers to hold aloft lighters, matches, and acetylene torches in some strange new ritual-istic gesture.

After rejecting several different ideas for a conceptual follow-up to *Who's Next* (*Whodunnit, Who's on First, Horton Hears a Who*), Townshend eventually settled on *Quadrophenia* (1973), an epic celebration of a new four-way sound that was revolutionizing the music industry. The band's next LP, *Who By Numbers* (1975), kept fans occupied for hours with its connect-the-dots cover, and con-tained a Top Forty hit in "Squeeze Box," about an instrument that was immediately added to Townshend's palette of guitars and unmerci-fully smashed at the end of gigs. *Who Are You* (1978), released shortly after drummer Keith Moon's death, was the Who's only serious attempt to confront the seventies head-on: "Sister Disco" paid tribute to Sister Sledge, and the LP's title track chronicled Townshend's gnawing feelings of irrelevance after being verbally attacked in an Irish pub by members of the Chieftains.

Three of the sixties other biggest names — Van Morrison, Eric Clapton, and the Grateful Dead — were able to sustain fan loyalty by simply going about their business whether anyone was paying attention or not. Morrison's most enduring album of the seventies, *Moondance* (1970), bounced from Ray Charles tributes ("These Dreams") to pastoral ballads ("And It Stoned Me") to the prescient title track, which Van choreographed during concerts by donning a sequined glove and sliding backwards across the stage on his hands and knees. Although the seventies was a decade full of Vans — Van Halen, Van Heflin, Van McCoy, Van Der Graaf Generator, the Van Patten family — none was as animated a presence as Mr. Morrison.

Eric Clapton joined Duane Allman, Bobby Whitlock, Clyde McPhatter, and Derek of "Cinammon" fame on Derek & the Domi-noes' *Layla and Other Assorted Love Songs* (1970), which reflected Clapton's growing Robert Johnson obsession on songs like the seven-minute title track, "Bell Bottom Blues," "Wedding Bell Blues," and "Supposedly That's Why They Call It the Blues." Johnson's presence was felt most vividly on *Layla* 's centerpiece, "George Harrison on My Trail," wherein Clapton described the dangers inherent in messing around with another man's woman.

The Grateful Dead began the decade with *Workingman's Dead*

26

and *American Beauty* (both 1970), two low-key albums highlighted by "Friend of the Devil," "Truckin'," and a new musical collaborator in Sammy Davis Jr. , who snapped his fingers through "Candyman" before turning it into a hit of his own in 1972. The Dead made their biggest news of the decade in 1978, when they hired Charlie's Angels to provide security for a free indoor concert at Studio 54. The result: one sprained ankle, seven minor scuffles on the dance floor, 475 hung over.

Speaking of the Dead, a much different route to immortality was taken by Jim Morrison, Janis Joplin, and Jimi Hendrix. The Doors' *L.A. Woman* (1971), released shortly before Morrison's death, featured a couple of Top Forty hits ("Love Her Madly" and "Riders on the Storm") and the rousing title track which still summons forth cries of "Mr. Mojo rising" among excitable teenagers. After *L.A. Woman,* the remaining Doors carried on in the spirit of Jim by securing a gig on *Let's Make a Deal* as Door #1, Door #2, and Door #3. Janis Joplin bid farewell with *Pearl* (1970), a posthumous release that featured a surprise number-one single in the Kris Kristofferson-penned "Me and Bobby McGee"; if only Janis had lived, it could have been her rolling around with Kris in the 1976 remake of *A Star Is Born.* Jimi Hendrix's final LP, *Cry of Love* (1971), was notable for songs like "Angel," "Astro Man," and "Belly Button Window," after which Jimi's legacy was kept alive by Funkadelic, Mahogany Rush, Montrose, and the Pat Travers Band.

Given Classic Rock radio's long-term fascination with *Who's Next, L.A. Woman,* and a few other post-Zager & Evans last gasps (e.g., C.C.R.'s *Cosmo's Factory,* Crosby, Stills, Nash & Young's *Déjà Vu,* and Santana's *Abraxas,* all of them 1970), it's surprising that the seventies got underway at all. They did, but we're not quite ready to take that monumental leap yet. First it's time for some quiet, introspective contemplation, a moment's pause before Ted Nugent, the DeFranco Family, the Alan Parsons Project, and a thousand other luminaries join hands to reinvent pop music from the inside out. Enjoy, because there'll be little time for reflection anywhere else.

Chapter 4

KRIS KRISTOFFERSON'LL MAKE YOU JUMP! JUMP!

"My poetry is urbanized and Americanized, but my music is influenced by the prairies. When I was a kid, my mother used to take me out to the fields to teach me bird calls."
—Joni Mitchell, 1974.

PEOPLE who write and sing the songs that make the whole world sing have been around since at least 410 B.C., when Plato picked up a harp and serenaded the object of his desire: "I'm begging you son, I'm down on my knees/Take my hand, forget Socrates." By 1971 A.D., singer-songwriters had become a dominant force in popular music, with a tranquil, nurturing approach that evoked the Association's "Never My Love" as much as it did Bob Dylan. Not all singer-songwriters were particularly cheery as they tiptoed into the seventies, but compared to Sly Stone, John Lennon, and others who felt they had to scream primally to be heard, the lonesome folkies of the period preferred to communicate with a whisper, a whimper, a lonely coo, or a dying quail.

Singer-songwriters had to follow a few rules in order to be part of the movement. First, they had to do both the singing and the songwriting—actually, they wrote the songs first and sang them later, but for some reason no one ever thought to call them songwriter-singers. Second, they were committed to keeping things simple: no makeup, no mellotrons, no Marshall stacks, no six-foot afros, no purple smokebombs, no overtures, no Giorgio Moroder remixes, no operators standing by, none of the things that would make the 1970s so fun, unique, and all but incomprehensible. Just a singer, a guitar, a piano, and a song. Now and again someone would throw in a little something extra like the sad and forlorn organ-grinder solo in Frank Mills' "Love Me, Love Me Love" (1972), but only if circumstances warranted. Third, singer-songwriters followed the lead of history's greatest self-absorbed neurotics — St. Augustine, Kierkegaard, Sylvia Plath, Woody Allen — by opening up their innermost secrets, the minutiae of their every last thought and desire and regret for public consumption and vicarious brooding. There was initially another rule, the controversial 'Tim rule,' that dictated all singer-songwriters must be named Tim —Tim Hardin, Tim Buckley, Tim Rose, Tiny Tim — but by 1970 it had run its course, with only the occasional latecomer like Mel & Tim, Timothy B. Schmit, and Tim Conway making an appearance.

The best place to fix the beginning of the singer-songwriter boom is James Taylor's *Sweet Baby James*, a February 1970 release that set the tone for all that followed. Whereas *Plastic Ono Band* had been conceived on a therapist's couch, Taylor went Lennon one better by addressing his experience in an institution on "Fire and Rain," *SBJ*'s standout track and one of the most beautiful songs of the decade: "Lord, I've seen fire and I've seen rain/I've seen flying pigs but remember I'm insane." His next major success was hitting number one with a cover of Carole King's "You've Got a Friend" (1971), after which he took old pop and R & B covers into the Top Ten three times: a duet with his wife Carly Simon on "Mockingbird" (1974), Marvin Gaye's "How Sweet It Is" (1975), and Jimmy Jones' "Handyman" (1977). Perhaps the key to James' divided psyche can be found hidden away in the title track of his *One Man Dog* LP (1972), a gentle lament for his loyal basset hound Bucky, whom Carly had recently replaced in James' heart: "You're a one man dog, but I'm a two-timin' man."

In one fell swoop, Carly Simon created an even bigger stir than her husband with "You're So Vain" (1973), a number-one single that had everyone madly trying to figure out who she was singing about: candidates included Mick Jagger, Warren Beatty, singing truckdriver

Red Sovine, New York Dolls' guitarist Syl Sylvain, and of course James himself. The controversy raged on for a few months, at which time James, Mick, Warren, Red, and Syl got together to record "You're So Vague,"a savage answer song that put the issue to rest. Carly's other great single was "Anticipation" (1971), which provided an ominous backdrop for a Heinz ketchup commercial, while her *No Secrets* LP (1973) had maybe the best cover art of the decade. There was an album inside too, but some buyers never got that far.

In the hands of Carole King, James' other female confidant, the singer-songwriter genre reached a level of popularity that would not be duplicated for the rest of the decade. When King released *Tapestry* (1971), she had already achieved considerable success as the co-writer (along with husband Gerry Goffin) of classic sixties hits for the Shirelles, the Righteous Brothers, Herman's Hermits, Tony Orlando, and countless others (with Tony being the only King-Goffin protégé adaptable and contemporary enough to last deep into the seventies). On *Tapestry* King reclaimed a couple of old hits ("Natural Woman" and "Will You Still Love Me Tomorrow"), added two new ones ("It's Too Late" and "So Far Away"), spent fifteen weeks atop *Billboard* 's album chart, outsold all Rolling Stones and ex-Beatles LPs released during the seventies, made a much better Upholstery Rock record than Genesis' "The Carpet Crawlers," and didn't even have to make a fool out of herself to do it.

Two of the era's key singer-songwriters emerged from Canada, a country with a rich heritage of identity crises and inferiority complexes, enough open space for everyone to co-exist in a state of complete aloneness, cold and snow and long winters to ensure cyclical depression for up to ten months a year, an endless supply of trees that could be cut down and fashioned into acoustic instruments of many varieties, and a shared sense of what it's like to grow up under the influence of *The Tommy Hunter Show*, *Don Messer's Jubilee*, *The Friendly Giant*, and other TV fare with strong singer-songwriter content. Alberta's Joni Mitchell came of age playing Toronto's coffeehouse circuit in the mid-sixties — legendary venues like Tim Horton's, Country Style, and Dunkin' Donuts — before eventually making her way to California. The early seventies saw Joni at the peak of her creative powers: *Blue* (1971) set new standards in the close analysis of male-female relationships (Joni resigning herself to the fact that "blue, blue, love is blue") and contained maybe her greatest song in "Carey"; "Electricity" and "You Turn Me On, I'm A Radio" from *For the Roses* (1972) were early examples of electro-pop; and *Court and Spark* (1974) had three sprightly Top Forty hits in "Raised on Robbery," "Help Me," and "Free Man in Paris." *Court and Spark* also featured the recklessly innovative blowing of saxophonist Tom Scott, a path Joni continued to pursue on tribute albums to Charles Mingus (*Mingus*, 1979), Walter Becker (*Walt*, 1980), and Doc Severinsen (*Doc*, 1981).

Neil Young, Canada's other leading singer-songwriter, had a résumé similar to Joni's. Born in Winnipeg, he moved to Toronto in the early sixties and hooked up with a band called the Mynah Birds (featuring Rick James, author of "Superfolk"), headed to California thereafter and joined Buffalo Springfield (which later split into Buffalo Tom and Rick Springfield), released a couple of late-sixties solo albums (1968's *Neil Young* and 1969's *Everybody Knows This Is Nowhere*), and found himself perfectly positioned as the seventies began. *After the Gold Rush* (1970) and *Harvest* (1972) — the former probably the best singer-songwriter album, the latter among the best-selling — were studies in paradox as Young obsessed about images and stories of old people: the "old man lying by the side of the road" on "Don't Let It Bring You Down"; an old woman on the cover of *Gold Rush* ; "Old Man" from *Harvest* ; and Neil's declaration "I'm gettin' old" on "Heart of Gold." Not until Henry Gross' sensitive ballad "Shannon" (1976) would a seventies pop star be so inappropriately named. Because Neil assembled a country-leaning band, the Stray Gators, to back him up on *Harvest* , many listeners felt the album lacked the immediacy of *Gold Rush*. "No way," insisted the always cryptic Neil, "we're doin' a thing called the crocodile rock."

The Rolling Stone Illustrated History of Rock & Roll traces the beginning of singer-songwriter madness to Simon and Garfunkel's 1967 score for *The Graduate*, so it shouldn't come as any surprise that three years later Paul was still right in the middle of things. Following the dissolution of Simon & Garfunkel in 1970, Simon continued on with no significant decline in popularity. His first release, 1972's *Paul Simon*, foreshadowed a day far into the future when he would captivate the rock audience with strange and wonderful new music from around the world: "Mother and Child Reunion" was reggae enough to earn Paul the nickname "Mr. Loverman" among Jamaicans, and "Me and Julio Down By the Schoolyard" had a strong baja-marimba feel to it, including some of the most rhythmically sophisticated whistling ever captured on record. In 1974, Paul had his first number-one single as a solo artist with "50 Ways To Leave Your Lover," which subsequently replaced "99 Bottles of Beer on the Wall" as the sing-along choice on school busses around the world.

Perhaps the oddest singer-songwriter bio belonged to Cat Stevens, who was strange because a) he was English, an anomaly in this genre; b) his first U.K. hit in 1967 was called "I Love My Dog," a big influence on James Taylor and quite shocking coming from a guy named Cat; and c) he surprised everyone when he quit the music business in 1979, declaring himself a disciple of Muhammad Ali and embarking on a quest to become featherweight champion of the world. A quick Cat scan reveals him to be a man of many personas: "Moon Shadow" (1971) was Cat the mystic, "Peace Train" (1971) was Cat the pacifist, "Morning Has Broken" (1972) was Cat the keyboard demon, and "Another Saturday Night" (1974) was Cat the classic soul stylist.

The early seventies wave of singer-songwriters was not generally renowned for its sense of humor, but at least three from its ranks, Randy Newman, Loudon Wainwright III, and Harry Nilsson, aspired to be the Lenny Bruces and Rusty Warrens of a new generation. On *12 Songs* (1970), *Sail Away* (1972), and *Good Old Boys* (1974), Newman placed himself in the shoes of everyone from rednecks to God to a naked man running down the street (1974's "Naked Man," his response to Ray Stevens' "The Streak"); actually, the naked man running down the street wasn't wearing any shoes, so Randy was a little out of his element there. After a three-year layoff, Newman returned with one of the decade's unlikeliest hit singles in "Short People" (1977). The song sparked protests all across North America, the biggest of which was led by child actor Ricky Schroeder. When it was pointed out to Ricky that he wasn't short at all, just young, he quickly withdrew his support.

Loudon Wainwright III — who should not be confused with

either Thurston Howell III or Dudley Do Right I — lucked into an equally fluky hit, 1973's "Dead Skunk," which many misheard as Loudon's attack on a fellow singer-songwriter who landed on the pop charts that same year with "Daisy a Day": "There's a Jud Strunk in the middle of the road/JUD STRUNK IN THE MIDDLE OF THE ROAD!"

As for Harry Nilsson, he got laughs in large part because of the way he looked: a hopelessly dissolute slob even by the standards of a decade that produced Elliot Gould, Billy Carter, Peter Falk, and John Belushi. *Nilsson Schmilsson* (1971) became a bestseller in the wake of a number-one ballad, "Without You," and the voodoo epic "Coconut," which was inspired by the bald man who did 7-Up's Uncola commercials at the time.

In 1972, Don McLean came up with one of the biggest and most compelling singer-songwriter hits of all, "American Pie." In highly ambitious and metaphoric images, "American Pie" used the plane-crash deaths of Buddy Holly, Ritchie Valens, and the Big Bopper as a springboard for McLean's declaration that rock and roll was dead (still a provocative thing to say in 1972). On his follow-up single, "Vincent," McLean declared Vincent Van Gogh dead, which proved much less controversial since most listeners agreed that Vince had been dead for one hundred years or so. By the time of *American Pie* 's third single, "Dreidel," where McLean declared his pet hamster Dreidel dead, everyone had pretty much lost interest.

Death also caught up with two of McLean's singer-songwriter colleagues, Jim Croce and Harry Chapin. Jim first gained notice as a novelty artist — a white Shaft, perhaps — with "You Don't Mess Around with Jim" (1972) and "Bad, Bad Leroy Brown" (1973), but after a fatal plane crash in September 1973, his record company concentrated on posthumous ballads such as "I Got a Name" (1973), "Time in a Bottle" (1973), and "I'll Have to Say I Love You in a Song" (1974). Always on the lookout for a good Zen challenge, George Harrison took Jim to heart and actually did spend three years trying to save time in a bottle, only to report back that "It can't be done, not unless you get something with an airtight twist-on cap."

Harry Chapin's first hit was "Taxi" (1972), and in 1974 he went to number one with "Cat's in the Cradle," a tribute to his favorite competitors in the singer-songwriter arena: "Cat's in the cradle and

Neil's got a tune/Carly and James comin' over real soon/Joni's bringin' beer but I don't know when/We'll get together then, yeah, you know we'll have a good time then."

In the first few years of the seventies, there were more singer-songwriters than anyone could count — Gordon Lightfoot, Eric Anderson, Kris Kristofferson, Dory Previn, John Prine, Melanie, Jerry Jeff ('J.J.') Walker, Jesse Winchester, Jonathan Edwards, Wild Man Fischer — and more than we have adequate space to detail here. Hopefully we've made it clear how radically sex roles changed during the singer-songwriter era, thanks to Carole King, Paul Simon, and Loudon Wainwright III. Without their pioneering efforts and those of their fellow singer-songwriters, there would never have been Suzanne Vega's "Luka," Tracy Chapman's "Fast Car," or Mr. Big's "To Be With You."

Before leaving the introspective realm completely behind, though, let's now take a look at what Jim Croce and James Taylor might have sounded like had they been black — which, of course, is what many people thought after hearing "Bad Bad Leroy Brown" and James' Marvin Gaye cover.

Chapter 5

I Want a Riot of My Own

"One reason that I'm on tour now is because I did feel the hearts of the people, and the pulse said, "Please let us hear you one more time."
— Marvin Gaye, 1974.

THE Beatles' breakup, *Who's Next*, and the singer-songwriter boom were an indelible part of what it felt like to be a pop fan in the early 1970s. No less significant, especially if you listened to Top Forty radio, were the dramatic changes overtaking the world of soul. Indeed, if there was any one branch of pop music that managed to carry itself with a degree of dignity in the seventies, the nod would have to go to the surge of black voices that flourished in the first half of the decade. For a while it seemed as if people like Al Green, the Chi-Lites, the Spinners, and Curtis Mayfield were maybe the last outpost of recognizable human behavior in an industry going haywire.

At the same time, however, those same people were part of a mini-drama that was every bit as implicated in the developing lunacy as all that surrounded it. Black artists found themselves seized by the impulse to do one of two things in the early seventies — start decrying every social ill imaginable, or curl up into a fetal ball and plead for sympathy, understanding, and a little sexual companionship. The legacy of this stark division within the ranks of soul singers can still be felt today: when a hardcore gangster rapper — the Snowman, for instance — follows up an angry jail song with one about romantic loss, he's replaying a schizophrenic polarity first exhibited by the Chi-Lites and company some twenty years ago.

A good place to begin this saga is inside the vast empire of Motown Records. The label that took flight in the early sixties as "The Sound of Young America" was, as that decade drew to a close, making its bid to be "The Slightly Muddled Consciousness-Raising-Hub of America" with the Supremes' "Love Child" (1968), the Temptations' "Cloud Nine" (1968), and other overt forays into black urban disintegration. Encouraged by the commercial success of these experiments, the Temps jumped full throttle into the sociology business: first in 1970 with "Psychedelic Shack," "Ball of Confusion," and "Ugena Za Ulimwengu"— a thinly disguised Afrocentric anagram for "A Zulu Gun-Naming Ewe"— and then a couple years later on "Papa Was a Rolling Stone," obvious cause for alarm after the guys got hold of some advance *Goats Head Soup* demos.

Other Motown acts caught the editorial bug as well: Edwin Starr's "War" (1970) had the most mortified "good *God*, y'all"s on record, the Undisputed Truth kept a wary eye peeled for "Smiling Faces Sometimes" (1971), and Junior Walker's "Way Back Home" (1971) was even adopted by the Symbionese Liberation Army as their official song — hard to say why, though there was a line about playing hide and seek that must have appealed to them.

Motown's two biggest contributors to the expanding consciousness of black pop were Marvin Gaye and Stevie Wonder. Marvin's *What's Going On* (1971), an indictment against the whole of Western Civilization, remains one of the decade's most famous recordings. The album was keyed by three Top Ten singles: the title track, "Inner City Blues (Make Me Wanna Holler)," and "Mercy Mercy Me (the Ecology)," with the latter setting into motion an eco-rock movement that swept through pop music (Betty Wright's "Clean Up Woman," 1972; the New York Dolls' "Trash," 1973; the Average White Band's "Pick up the Pieces," 1975). Stevie's "Superstition" (1972) and "Livin' for the City" (1973) were bleak warnings of imminent collapse, and on "You Haven't Done Nothin'" (1974) he issued the most pointed attack on Richard Nixon since CSNY's "Ohio" (1970).[1] Stevie even threw down a challenge to his contemporaries with 1973's "Higher Ground": "Cher, keep on sharing/Bee Gees, keep on being/Raiders, just stop raiding."

Enter Shaft: John Shaft, that is, the only brother who won't cop out, the private dick who gets more chicks, and the smooth-loving/ fist-clenching/sharp-dressing/eyebrow-arching/Man-distrusting hero of the 1971 film of the same name. As played by Richard Roundtree, Shaft walked a perilous tightrope between women who wanted to nurture his introspective side by cuddlin', nuzzlin', and humpin' him all night long — and verily, Shaft did oblige them — and the daily grind of low-life dope dealers, ghetto squalor, and strident black militants that chipped away at his soul and invaded his space. And, of course, there was "the Man"— not that man, and not that man either (we know that man, he's a nice guy), but *the* Man, the big Man, Whitey Ford — er, Whitey Herzog — check that, plain old Whitey! To get his head unmessed, Shaft spent most of the film walking the streets of New York — and walking, and walking, and walking a little bit more — while the soundtrack blared Isaac Hayes' theme music of a couple of flutes, the "Chopsticks" of fuzzed-up funk riffs, and a basso profundo rap that was enough to make James Earl Jones cower. *Shaft* proved to be enormously popular with black and white audiences alike, and the 'blaxploitation' cycle of films that was so integral to the look, content, and most of all shtick of early-seventies soul was launched.

The big score (just to keep in the vernacular) was Curtis Mayfield's soundtrack for *Superfly* (1972), which reversed the angle on *Shaft:* instead of an agent of the law caught between quixotic romance and oppressive despair, *Superfly* examined the life of 'Priest,' a dope dealer caught in the same existential vice-grip. Mayfield came down hard on Priest in songs like "Pusher Man," "Freddie's Dead," and the title track, but true to formula there was still time enough for some bubblebath frolics on "Give Me Your Love." Incidentally, just as the Man lurked in the shadows of the asphalt jungle presided over by Priest and Shaft, the Woman played her part too: both men had a

---

[1] The president was all ears, tendering his resignation within two weeks of Stevie's diatribe: " I always thought I'd have the support of the rhythm and blues brotherhood. If they're bailing out on me, I know my time is short."

white lover to complement his black girlfriend, thereby accentuating his sensual needs and getting under Whitey's skin just a little bit more in the bargain.

With *Superfly* , *What's Going On*, and Sly's *Riot* leading the way — well, Sly was scheduled to lead the way, but he forgot to show up that day — black artist after black artist began to step up to the podium and announce, "Hey America, Brady Bunch or no Brady Bunch, I ain't havin' much fun." One of the best was California's War, who had earlier shared billing with Eric Burdon on the totally bizarre "Spill the Wine" (1970). After ditching Eric, War joined the anomie parade with "Slippin' Into Darkness" and "The World Is a Ghetto" (both 1972), heroic laments that were gloomy beyond time, space, and *Bullwinkle*'s Mr. Peabody character. War went on to bigger hits such as "The Cisco Kid" (1973) and the wonderfully serene "Summer" (1976), but they're most remembered today for 1975's "Low Rider," a much-sampled celebration of that year's National Soap Box Derby. For "Low Rider" and much else, let's hear a rousing "good *God*, y'all!" for War.

Sometimes the politicization of black pop took on a decidedly spiritual bent, possibly rooted in gospel traditions but more likely reflecting the profound influence of George Harrison's "My Sweet Lord." Johnny Nash ("I Can See Clearly Now,"1972), the Staple Singers ("I'll Take You There," 1972), and Bill Withers ("Lean On Me," 1972) all dared to look beyond the encroaching mayhem long enough to envision a light at the end of the tunnel, with the Staples even offering the sanctuary of a place where "there ain't no smilin' faces"— either a reference to the Undisputed Truth song, or a complimentary pass to see Barbara Streisand and Ryan O' Neal in *What's Up Doc?* .

The Chi-Lites ("Give More Power to the People," 1971) and the Dramatics ("Whatcha See Is Whatcha Get," 1971) also dabbled in social discourse, but here the focus begins to shift to introverted, vulnerable, forlorn puppy-dog Romeos who were too busy getting in touch with their loneliness, and too overcome by romantic longing, to worry about a little gunfire in the streets. The Dramatics' "In the Rain" (1972) was a virtual manifesto for the sensitive-guy set, complete with ultra-moody wah-wah, lots of desolate wind around the edges, and an abandoned man who "may start cryin'" on the mic — not for the world, though, and not for future generations either, but for himself, like any self-pitying martyr. The Chi-Lites similarly turned to mush on "Have You Seen Her" (1971) and "Oh Girl" (1972), first because their woman left them and later because she *could theoretically leave* . "Have you ever seen such a helpless man?" whispered the Chi-Lites' Eugene Record as "Oh Girl" faded away; on the evidence of "A Lonely Man" (1972) and "The Coldest Days of My Life" (1972), Eugene was actually boasting — Say it loud, I'm a simp and I'm proud!

Critic Vince Aletti dubbed this new kind of male persona 'neoclassical soul,' and its other leading practitioners were Al Green, the Spinners, and the Stylistics. Green, one of the early-seventies greatest singles artists, explored eternal domestic bliss on "Let's Stay Together" (1971), "I'm Still In Love With You" (1972), and "You Ought To Be With Me" (1972). Al eventually became so caught up in the rapture of love, he mistook a pot of steaming hot grits his girlfriend heaved at him in 1974 for some new kind of erotic foreplay. The Spinners proudly played the sap on "I'll Be Around" (1972), tremulously wondered "Could It Be I'm Falling In Love" (1972), played footsie with Dionne Warwick on "Then Came You" (1974), and pretty much threw themselves at the mercy of any woman in sight.

The cuddliest teddy bears of all were the Stylistics, who took unabashed male vulnerability into a new dimension on "You Are Everything" (1971), "Betcha By Golly, Wow" (1972),[2] and "You Make Me Feel Brand New" (1974). Turning our Isaac Hayes/James Earl Jones comparison on its head, Stylistics' lead singer Russell Thompkins Jr. brandished a falsetto that probably made even James Taylor want to pummel him inside-out. But to all of us who were afraid of our own shadow in those days, Russell was the emotional compass against which we measured our quiet burden of sorrow.

Neoclassical was everywhere in the early seventies. Two of the best early examples were the Moments' "Love on a Two-Way Street" and the Delfonics' "Didn't I (Blow Your Mind This Time)," both from 1970. The following year, the Persuaders made a major breakthrough by having their girlfriends beat them up on "Thin Line Between Love & Hate." Eventually childlike metaphor took over: Al Wilson regressed

---

[2.] Go ahead guys — try impressing a girl by saying "betcha by golly wow" and see what happens.

to his kindergarten days on "Show and Tell" (1973), Blue Magic went to the circus on "Sideshow" (1974), and the Dynamic Superiors saved up their pennies, nickels, and dimes on "Shoe Shoe Shine" (1974), primarily so they could whisper the words "shoe shoe shine" every time they got to the chorus. Occasionally, as on Love Unlimited's "Walking in the Rain With the One I Love" and Brighter Side of Darkness's "Love Jones" (both 1972), soul ballads entered the realm of pure loopiness.

It would be simplifying matters greatly to say that all soul music in the early seventies was either militant or neoclassical. There was also lots of black pop of a more traditional style, the kind that Motown made in the mid-sixties, and some of the most exciting singles of the day fell into this third non-category. The biggest success story of the period was Motown's newest sensation, the Jackson 5, owners of four number-one singles in 1970: "I Want You Back," "ABC," "The Love You Save," and "I'll Be There." The group was led by an eleven-year-old whirling dervish named Michael, who in *Teenbeat* magazine that year enumerated his three main goals in life: to bring peace and harmony through his music to nations in every corner of the world; to do a live ninety-minute interview with his favorite television personality, Joey Bishop; and to make enough money one day to purchase the Badfinger song catalogue. Young Michael only got to fulfil one of his dreams, but how many of us accomplish even that?

Complementing the Jackson 5 on Top Forty playlists was an abundance of terrific black pop. A quick look at 1970 alone turns up some impressive examples: the Chairmen of the Board's "Give Me Just a Little More Time," the Five Stairsteps' "O-o-h Child," the 5th Dimension's "One Less Bell To Answer," Smokey Robinson & the Miracles' "Tears of a Clown," and Honey Cone's highly classified "Wants Ads," which described primitive mating rituals in the days before 976-lines came into being. Best of all was Freda Payne's "Band of Gold," a sparkling account of honeymoon impotence — as far as we know, Freda's voice has still not been heard at a single wedding reception.

And so it went during this memorable transition period for soul music. But whether the action took place on the streets, in the hot-tub, or over by the finger-painting center, one fast-rising record label

stood front and center the whole way. It was a label that encompassed the most sublime heights, the silliest depths, and a factory-like
efficiency that recalled Motown in the mid-sixties. It changed music,
it changed history, and it changed mankind. Yes, this is your cue to
read the next chapter.

Chapter 6

Do a Little Dance, Make a Little Love

" Some people laugh at people who try to be righteous. Striving
to be righteous in an unrighteous system is the hardest thing to do"
— Kenny Gamble liner notes, 1977.

By 1972, Motown Records had effectively relinquished whatever claim it once held to being the vital center of popular black music
in America. There are a variety of graphs and charts we could call upon
to prove this, but to save time we'll simply point out that Motown had
two number-one hits in 1972, and one of them, Michael Jackson's
"Ben," was a love song about a rat. Although Aerosmith ("Rats in the
Cellar") and Captain & Tennille ("Muskrat Love") would later achieve
some success in this exciting field, a romantic attraction to rodents is
a leading indicator that something is seriously amiss.

Black pop was undergoing a major geographical shift in 1972,
one that had been foreshadowed a year earlier when the Spinners left
Motown for Philadelphia. The Stylistics and the Delfonics were already
thriving in Philly at the time, and revitalized veterans Wilson Pickett
("Don't Let the Green Grass Fool You") and Joe Simon ("Drowning In
the Sea of Love") had just cut hit singles there. Nineteen seventy-two
was also the beginning of a mini-dynasty for the Philadelphia Flyers,
who were spurred on by scoring sensation Bobby Clarke and singer

Kate Smith's fiery versions of "God Bless America" before each game. The City of Brotherly Love, aka the City of Fabian Forte, was suddenly the place to be: it seemed as if people all over the world were joining hands and forming an unstoppable human chain, a powerful vehicle to transport the hopes and aspirations of an entire generation, a love train if you will.

Conducting this runaway choo-choo was largely the province of Kenny Gamble, Leon Huff, and Thom Bell, the driving forces behind Philadelphia International Records, a label launched by Gamble and Huff in 1971. PIR soon became associated with a style that was hyperbolic, symphonic, and blustery, and was the bridge that connected classic soul to the Salsoul Orchestra, the Temptations to Wild Cherry, Neil Armstrong to Evel Knievel, *Room 222* to *Welcome Back Kotter,* and Allen Ludden to Chuck Barris.

Philly International didn't make much noise during its first year of operation, but in July of 1972 it let loose with a couple of growls that characterized the label's attack in the years that followed. First up was Harold Melvin & the Blue Notes' "I Miss You," in which lead singer Teddy Pendergrass repeated the title 763 times over the course of eight-and-a-half overwhelming minutes. It wasn't enough to get his woman back, but it was an impressive display of Zen prayer technique anyway. Leapfrogging over it all the way to number one was the O'Jays' "Backstabbers," an extension of the paranoia found on "Smiling Faces" and "Whatcha See Is Whatcha Get" into the realm of pure dementia. As an added bonus, purchasers of "Backstabbers" received a complete set of Ginsu knives and a bumper sticker declaring "YOU BETTER BEWARE."

Two of the label's signature songs appeared toward the end of 1972, the Blue Notes' "If You Don't Know Me By Now" and Billy Paul's "Me and Mrs. Jones," over-the-top domestic dramas that pitted Teddy's exhortations of marital fidelity on the one hand against a little friendly backstabbing from Billy on the other. The O'Jays kicked off 1973 with "Love Train" (nice title!), a bubbly call for universal brotherhood that paired up well with "Shifty, Shady, Jealous Kind of People" from the same album. The Gamble & Huff philosophy was starting to take shape: all we have to do is get those of us who are shifty together with those who are shady, mix in a solid block of jealous types for variety, and the world will be a much more amicable place in which to live. If we can go the extra mile and reach out to the backstabbers, we'll pretty much be in Shangri-La.

The Blue Notes and the O'Jays — and Kate Smith too, who continued to belt out wilder and wilder versions of "God Bless America" — quickly emerged as the big guns around Philadelphia, huffing and puffing their way through a series of epic hits. In no time at all Teddy Pendergrass lost his girl ("The Love I Lost," 1973), his friends and social standing ("Where Are All My Friends," 1974), and his faith in government, country, and the whole social order ("Bad Luck," 1975, with its distraught summary of Watergate —"He did *resign*, y'all!").

Gamble and Huff did most of their proselytizing via the O'Jays, hyping the group's lyrics, album concepts, and liner notes with a spiritually complex love-generation vibe rivaled only by Irwin Allen's production of *The Towering Inferno* for apocalyptic fervor. The O'Jays railed against rampant greed on "For the Love of Money," tackled slavery on "Ship Ahoy" (1973), warned of global warming on "Sunshine Pt. II," (1974), and celebrated the importance of second-cousins-twice-removed on "Family Reunion," (1975). They even did a message song about how songs need to have messages, 1976's "Message in the Music" (cf. the Bee Gees' "I've Gotta Get a Message to You," the Police's "Message in a Bottle," and the Five Americans' "Western Union" for other important message songs). The O'Jays peaked with "I Love Music" in 1975, maybe the best single of the whole decade.

Philadelphia International's undisputed anthem, however, was "T.S.O.P." (1974), an almost wordless showcase for the label's house musicians that was commissioned by Don Cornelius as the theme for *Soul Train*. Dubbing themselves MFSB for the occasion — Malcontent and Frustrated Second Bananas — the band roared through a sideways version of "Love Train"'s instrumental track, while a trio of females blurted out "M-F-S-B, everyone's accusing me!" every so often. "T.S.O.P." single-handedly defined 'The Sound of Philadelphia,' even if twenty years later we still can't figure out what the title's acronym stood for.

Later that same year, the Three Degrees (the trio who provided the blurting on "T.S.O.P.") had their own Top Ten hit with "When Will I See You Again." Never a favorite at *Ms.* magazine, the Degrees were accused of setting back feminism three or four hundred years; they *oohed* and *aahed* like modern-day Betty Boops, made frequent references in their songs to a woman's basic incompleteness without a man, proudly offered themselves up as love slaves, and wore a variety of see-through sequined gowns that were — hang on while we double-check our files — yes, that were absolutely uncalled for.

With "T.S.O.P.," "I Love Music," and "Bad Luck," Philadelphia International was clearly on to something new: lengthy, trance-inducing dance tracks that the public took to in a big way. Meanwhile, over on the set of *Welcome Back Kotter,* a sense of imminent adventure was in the air. Could it be that this new kind of music and Arnold Horshack were destined to make history together? Unfortunately, our own chronology's out of wack at this point, so we have to back up to 1970 again and save the answer for later.

Chapter 7

GORILLAS IN THE MIST

"I was standing out at the back of the club between sets and this guy says, 'Is it true you've gone insane?' I said, 'What?' And he says, 'The word's out on you that you're mad, didn't you hear?' I just shook my head, 'I dunno.'"
— Ozzy Osbourne, 1971.

As far as pop music went, the 1970s took its first significant step toward establishing an identity with the advent of heavy metal. After all, what could possibly be dopier than the sight of four long-haired monsters pounding away on the same grueling riff for what seemed like an eternity? Three things, actually: the sight of 40,000 wayward souls gathered together under one roof, bobbing their heads up and down in unison; the intense academic debate among concerned citizens over the moral, socioeconomic, and philological worth of heavy metal; and, of course, there was the music.

You've no doubt heard every pro and con heavy metal argument in existence, so we'll skip the preliminaries and get right down to the fundamental question of who invented metal. It's a highly contentious issue, but archaeologists usually point first to the song structures and affirmative action lyrics of 1930s Delta blues, then jump ahead a couple decades to Fats Domino, the first truly heavy rock artist; from there they go to the mid-sixties British Riff-Rock Invasion of the Kinks, the Who, the Yardbirds, and Gerry & the Pacemakers, and then over to Jimi Hendrix and Cream, who brought the concept of 'interesting guitar solo' and 'really interesting drum solo' to pop music. Finally they end up at Steppenwolf, Blue Cheer, and Iron Butterfly, whose "In-A-Gadda-Da-Vida" was only twelve minutes shorter than a half-hour sitcom. Perhaps the last word in this conundrum belongs to the Staple Singers, who declared in 1971 that "Heavy Makes You Happy (So Children, Please Stop Arguing Over Who Invented Metal)."

What *is* indisputable is the pre-eminence of metal's most popular group, Led Zeppelin. Formed in 1968 by ex-Yardbirds guitarist Jimmy Page, Zeppelin's vast popularity and equally immense disrepute was partly due to the many legends that engulfed them: Page's dalliance with necromancy, Ouija boards, and Doug Henning worship; the round-the-clock adventures of Goldilocks-in-drag singer Robert Plant; and the band's notorious behavior in hotels around the world, which saw them order room service when they didn't even want it, steal soap, towels, and phonebooks by the truckload, and check out without ever once making their beds.

Although Led Zeppelin played an exotic game of musical chairs all decade (country blues, Middle Eastern meditations, touches of reggae and calypso, pilgrimages to the land of Joni), they were primarily revered for colossal masterworks like "Whole Lotta Love" (1969), "Black Dog" (1971), "The Ocean" (1973), and "Houses of the Holy" (1975), songs that remain the best arguments heavy metal has ever made for itself. The most popular Zeppelin track of all was 1971's "Stairway to Heaven," taken from their hugely popular fourth LP, confusingly known as either *Led Zeppelin IV, Zo-So* (in honor of Hans, their German sound technician who declared it a "zo-so album"), *The Runes Album*, or *The Album That Followed Led Zeppelin III and Preceded Houses of the Holy* . Besides being the central reason for the existence of Spinal Tap, backward masking committees, and Stryper, "Stairway" was the first encounter most rock fans had with the word 'hedgerow,' and, until Van McCoy's "The Hustle" came along in 1975, the heaviest song of the seventies with a score for flute. Zeppelin remained at the top of the metal pile throughout the seventies, with each of their albums going multi-multi-platinum, but they had to call it quits in 1980 after drummer John Bonham was fatally wounded while counting up to forty.

Two other British heavy metal acts, Black Sabbath and Deep Purple, pursued less eclectic paths to the unquiet grave, inspiring in the process even more animosity from the non-metal world than Led Zeppelin. Sabbath was guided by Ozzy Osbourne and his wife Harriet, and for the duration of the seventies they cast a spell over fans as powerful as Dr. Tongue's *3-D House of Stewardesses*. Their most popular album, 1971's *Paranoid*, featured a true classic in the speedy, hooky, absurd title track, and also some gossip fodder for *Circus* magazine re "Fairies Wear Boots": were they referring to Bryan Ferry, Nancy Sinatra or Boots Randolph? The LP's definitive moment came on "War Pigs," heavy metal's answer to Edwin Starr's "War" and the Beatles' "Piggies": "Generals gathered in their masses/Just like witches at black masses/Marx predicted warring classes/Would you like some backstage passes?"

Deep Purple emerged from a late sixties psychedelic background to release *Machine Head* in 1972, a collection of pipe-organ mayhem that was beloved for techno-thrash numbers like "Highway Star," "Space Truckin'," and "Smoke On the Water," the latter a horrifying story of a marshmallow roast gone awry. Built around a memorable four-note riff, "Smoke" was Purple's biggest hit, and it quickly became the first song required of every teenager whose parents had bought him a guitar from the Sears catalogue (followed in short order by "Stairway to Heaven"'s acoustic intro, the complete works of the Mahavishnu Orchestra, and Wagner's *Der Ring des Nibelungen* played backwards at twice the speed). Also noteworthy from the Purple canon were "My Woman From Tokyo" (1972), a searing valentine to Mika of the Sadistic Mika Band, and the heavy religious/birthday-cake symbolism of *Burn*'s (1974) cover photo.

American heavy metal started out as sludgy as the British version, but by mid-decade it was as buoyant as Petula Clark or the Lovin' Spoonful. Three of the finest early seventies metal bands, the Stooges, the MC5, and Grand Funk Railroad, hailed from the greater Detroit area. The Stooges, who released three of the most chaotic LPs ever recorded, had a peculiar obsession with naming songs after the year in which they were written. There was "1969" from *The Stooges,*

"1970" from *Fun House*, and then *Raw Power*'s "1973," with its immortal second verse: "Well last year I was 25/Got to meet the Jackson 5/Now I'm gonna be 26/Gonna set my sights on Styx." The MC5 caused an immediate sensation with "Kick Out the Jams" (1969), an inflammatory number they copped from sixties psychedelic band the Peanut Butter Conspiracy, but by the time of *Back in the U.S.A.* (1970) they were helping to point American metal in the direction of Little Richard and Chuck Berry (both of whom they covered), the Beach Boys (they "Sis-Boom-Rah"ed about high school), and old Annette Funicello and Frankie Avalon movies ("Teenage Lust").

Grand Funk Railroad started out as archetypal early-seventies journeymen, touring incessantly, quacking at length about their love for the kids, and chugging their way through primordial arena slop like "Inside Lookin' Out" (1970) and "Footstompin' Music" (1972). Then in one of the wiser career moves in metal history, the band completely made themselves over in 1973: they dropped the Railroad from their name ("It might help us establish a strong R&B base," said lead singer Mark Farner), enlisted the technical expertise of Todd Rundgren (who that same year handled production and/or reproduction for the New York Dolls, Fanny, and *Playboy* Playmate Bebe Buell), and had their 'fros enlarged and their toenails manicured. The strategy clicked with "We're an American Band" (1973) and a cover of Little Eva's "The Locomotion" (1974), both number-one hits. "Give us more train songs," they pleaded with Rundgren, "we like trains." The formula worked for a couple more years, highlighted by smashing covers of "Chattanooga Choo Choo" and "The Little Engine That Could," but by 1976 the Funk was pretty much derailed. In honor of their nine Top Forty hits and twenty million albums sold, the Parker Bros. rezoned the Monopoly board and created a "Grand Funk Railroad" deed.

By the mid-seventies, there were all sorts of American metal acts knocking out Top Forty hits that sounded just fine in a beat-up Dodge Duster with souped-up mag wheels and a pair of fuzzy dice dangling from the rear-view mirror. Boston's Aerosmith was originally labeled a 'poor man's Rolling Stones' because singer Steve Tyler and guitarist Joe Perry bore a suspicious resemblance to the two guys from the 'real Rolling Stones' (similar mix-ups were reported on the set of *Escape from Planet of the Apes*). They made it into the Top Forty six times anyway, including two of metal's most sparkling creations: "Sweet Emotion" (1975), a touching invitation to a groupie that put the fear of God into the U.S. Department of Health and Human Services ("I'll take you backstage, you can drink from my glass"), and "Walk This Way" (1976), which had so many syllables per second it was later remade by Run-D.M.C. as part of the mid-eighties skiffle-rap boom.

Boston (who was not from Aerosmith) struck a power chord among introspective metal fans with their self-titled debut album, a Bicentennial collection that sold millions. The group's reclusive leader, Tom Scholtz, had a degree in mechanical engineering, so it stands to reason that their best songs ("More Than a Feeling" and "Long Time") were a unique combination of love, good timing, and advanced vector analysis.

California's Van Halen popped up late in the decade with two smash albums (1978's *Van Halen* and 1979's *Van Halen II*), two of the seventies' greatest AOR hits ("Jamie's Cryin'," 1978, and "Dance the Night Away," 1979), and a couple of very charismatic frontmen in Eddie Van Halen and David Lee Roth, the Martin & Lewis of heavy metal. Eddie's trademark was a whole new inventory of squelching sounds attained by massaging the neck of his instrument with both hands at once (a technique later perfected by Pee Wee Herman), while Dave was nothing short of a Masters & Johnson case study.

Speaking of penis substitutes, metal's 'No Girls Allowed (Well, You Know What We Mean)' rule was finally overturned in the mid-seventies by the Runaways, a teen-queen outfit who were able to build on earlier, less successful attempts by Birtha, Fanny, and the GTOs. The inward-looking "Cherry Bomb" (1977) was the Runaways' only quasi-hit, but they'll always be remembered for launching the careers of Joan Jett and Lita Ford, as well as for providing inspiration for at least a dozen Linda Blair TV vehicles. Much more popular was Heart, a Seattle band that featured sisters Ann and Nancy Wilson commanding untold legions of adolescent tongue-waggers to commit unspeakable acts of pulmonary arrest. The group virtually invented today's exciting 'SubPop Sound' with "Magic Man" and "Crazy on You" (both 1976), and on "Barracuda" (1977) they easily outdistanced Led Zeppelin's "Moby Dick" (1969) and Dickie Goodman's "Mr. Jaws" (1975) for hardest-rocking fish-metal ever.

This will surprise you, but heavy metal also got very clownish at times during the seventies. New York's Blue Oyster Cult pioneered 'thinking man's metal,' an important breakthrough in human history, when they elicited musical, lyrical, and production input from rock critics Sandy Pearlman, Richard Meltzer, Patti Smith, and Gene Shalit. The result was *Tyranny and Mutation* (1973), "Dominance and Submission" (1974), "Golden Age of Leather" (1977), and other over-the-top silliness that was nonetheless swallowed whole by many. "(Don't Fear) the Reaper" (1976) was BOC's biggest hit, a terrific centre-of-the-mindish journey back to the Amboy Dukes. The Dicta-tors, who could be classified as 'friends of BOC,' explored the deep psychic connections between metal, wrestling, surfing, and Jewish-African brotherhood on *Go Girl Crazy!* (1976), one of the funniest and liveliest albums of the decade. And then there was ex-Amboy Duke Ted Nugent ('The Motor City Madman' to his fan club, 'Dances With Caribou' to his wife), as famous for his achievements with a bow and arrow as for sentimental favorites like "Cat Scratch Fever" (1977) and "Yank Me, Crank Me" (1978). Ted even captured the U.S. National Squirrel Shooting Archery Contest in 1974, quite impressive when you consider how difficult it is to paint tiny concentric circles on the backs of nervous squirrels.

No survey of heavy metal would be complete without a look at its massive worldbeat base: Australia, the Netherlands, Canada, Zaire, Togo — there wasn't a country in the world that didn't have its own metal heroes. Australia's greatest contribution (at least until the arrival of Men at Work) was AC/DC, a highly rechargeable unit that did their country proud with "Dirty Deeds Done Dirt Cheap" (1976) and "Highway to Hell" (1979). The group's chief assets were singer Bon Scott, an uncanny Tasmanian Devil soundalike, and guitarist Angus Young, who changed the course of rock history by donning a pair of shorts — next time you have to look at more of Axl Rose than you really care to see, be sure to drop Angus a thank-you card. Golden Earring rode out of the Netherlands with the 150 m.p.h. "Radar Love" (1974), a worldwide hit about the controversial *M*A*S*H* episode in which the 4077's lugubrious dispatcher tries to seduce Corporal Klinger. Canada was home to a number of metal mutants (Moxy, Triumph, Goddo, Max Webster, Hagood Hardy), but the only one able to leap across the border and headline foreign hockey arenas was Rush, an enigmatic trio identified with the philosophical writings of Ayn Landers. Rush had pretty much left metal behind by the time of 1976's *2112*, however, becoming so tangled up in concepts, precepts, forceps, and triceps (not to mention percussion overkill to rival John Phillip Sousa) that no one quite knew *what* they were anymore. A major clue was provided when one of the little pods in 1978's *Invasion of the Body Snatchers* let out a high-pitched squeal that sounded just like Geddy Lee.

So where did it all end? Needless to say, it didn't. Metal went into retreat for a while in the late seventies, knocked into hiding by disco, new wave, and the Little River Band, but it came back big in the early eighties. Then it went away again, then it did some handstands, now it's back for good as a bunch of complicated sub-genres: speed-metal, death-metal, Nerf-metal, Smurf-metal, Christian-metal, pagan-metal, disco-metal, art-metal, Art Deco-metal, so on and so forth. The permutations are still being sorted out.

Chapter 8

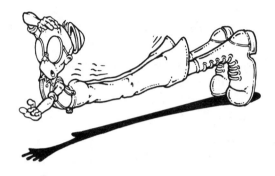

Judy in Disguise (With Glasses)

"I know I look ridiculous sometimes, absolutely idiotic,
but remember, when I started, I was quite rotund."
— Elton John, 1976.

Looking at pop music during the mid-seventies, it's no exaggeration to say that all roads, yellow brick or otherwise, eventually lead to Elton John. Elton was like the all-seeing, all-knowing, all-omniscient eyes of Doctor T.J. Eckleburg in F. Scott Fitzgerald's *The Great Gatsby*, especially as Doctor T.J.'s eyes peered out from "a pair of enormous yellow spectacles" just like the kind Elton used to wear. Mind you, plain yellow would never have cut it for Doctor E.J., they'd have to have been candy-coated pink-and-yellow gizmos with trails of neon purple smoke shooting out from each arm. Elton was glam, he was K-Tel, he was Philly International, he was a singer-songwriter supreme, he was arty as all get-out, he was the whole mid-seventies package in a jumbo-sized human gong show of bottomless variety and twisted complexity. In the arena of shameless public spectacledom, he was king.

Elton began in the mid-sixties as the pianist for British blues group Bluesology. After Bluesology split up in 1967, a *New Musical*

Express ad led him to hook up with struggling lyricist Bernie Taupin, launching the songwriting team that would crank 'em out mercilessly over the next decade. Their method of collaboration has passed into legend: Bernie driving himself to get every last word exactly right, sometimes spending up to a full hour on a set of lyrics, almost as long as it took the Trashmen to compose "Surfin' Bird"; sending those words by carrier pigeon to Elton, who then juggled half-notes, quarter-notes, and three-sevenths notes till Bernie's syllables developed natural rhythm; all the while making sure they never actually saw each other because, well, you've seen them.

After a few months of diddling around with what Elton later termed "all that Windmills of Your Mind and Canyons of Your Bowels stuff" (take *that*, Joni Mitchell), the John-Taupin team earned their breakthrough American hit with "Your Song" in 1970. This first incarnation of Elton, which also accounted for "Levon," "Tiny Dancer" (both 1971), and about every third hit thereafter, showcased a sensitive, frightened, imploringly earnest romantic, sort of James Taylor with a candelabrum and a string section to keep him company. Subsequent ballads like "Daniel" (1973), "Don't Let the Sun Go Down On Me" (1974), and "Someone Saved My Life Tonight" (1975) were Sammy Maudlin to the core, as integral to the development of Adult Contemporary as Olivia Newton-John, Paul Anka, or anyone else you could name from the Nat King Cole wing of seventies pop. Of course, the richer and more outlandish Elton got, the more Bernie's lyrics were liable to stretch credulity beyond the pale — "You can't plant me in your penthouse, I'm goin' back to my plough" from "Goodbye Yellow Brick Road" (1973) was a little hard to accept from a multi-millionaire wearing a nine-foot top hat and a silver lamé jumpsuit.

We digress — that was Elton #1, Elton the introvert, a throwback to his sheltered schoolboy upbringing and a stark contrast to the intrepid showman who started to take shape on 1972's "Honky Cat," a Joplinesque (Scott, not Janis) tale of botched alchemy that foreshadowed the chemical change about to overtake Elton himself. It was this second version of Elton that became a consuming presence in the midseventies: a guy who was just too cheerfully over-the-top fruit loops for any faction of the splintering pop audience to resist, and a true genius at taking three-minute songs that were nothing more than little stabs at happiness and transforming them into gleaming, larger-than-life pop statements about time, love, and gender-benderness — all of them set to the runaway beat of electric music and solid walls of sound.

Take "Crocodile Rock" (1972), Elton's cryptically ebullient salute to fifties rock and roll. Alluding to heroes like Bill Haley ("See You Later, Alligator") and Screamin' Jay Hawkins ("Alligator Wine") on one level, the song's cheesy kazoo ambience and Bernie's typically incongruous lyrics — can you picture Elton skipping stones down by the old swimming hole? — instead combined to give it the urgency of such nostalgia heavyweights as Sha Na Na's Bowser and Potsie from *Happy Days*. As for the dance that "Crocodile Rock" took its name from, one could only guess: presumably it involved laying down on your stomach and flapping your jaws voraciously. While some amphibian lovers opted for swamp land in Florida, the rest of us grabbed hold of Elton and made "Crocodile Rock" his first number-one single.

Elton's most famous LP, *Goodbye Yellow Brick Road* (1973), really sent him and Bernie spinning into the stratosphere. True to the *Sgt. Pepper/Tommy* agenda, Bernie had already used the LPs *Tumbleweed Connection* (1971) and *Don't Shoot Me, I'm Only the Piano Player* (1972) for a Wild West thematic hook, picked up from years of watching *Gunsmoke* reruns dubbed into Cockney. On *Yellow Brick Road* he let his theme mania run wild by taking on the greatest me-myself-and-I-decade subject of all, how tough it was to remain true to one's inner self when eight or nine solar systems revolved around you (not to mention the trauma unique to the rock star end of public service, having to pretend you liked Don Kirshner of *Rock Concert* renown). The autobiographical element of *Yellow Brick Road* fades at this late date, but the album did produce two of Elton's most irresistible singles: "Saturday Night's Alright For Fighting," a barroom blitz that should have shamed the Rolling Stones into handing over their instruments (no such luck — "Angie" shot past it on the charts), and "Bennie and the Jets", which one-upped David Bowie's Ziggy Stardust as effectively as Elton's earlier "Rocket Man" (1972) lunar-eclipsed "Space Oddity."

From 1974 to 1976, Elton's commercial clout and iconic resonance were astonishing — he was the world's number-one celebrity in terms of recognition factor ("Egads!" being the universal product code for EI), and everything he threw up there in the way of records managed to stick and then multiply exponentially. Like any true seventies megastar, Elton pilfered equipment from other people's playgrounds shamelessly: some more Stones ("The Bitch Is Back," 1974), some Gamble and Huff ("Philadelphia Freedom," Elton's 1975 tribute to tennis),[1] a little roots reggae for Elton's Rastafarian fans ("Island Girl," 1975), a blast of Captain & Tennille for mom and dad ("Don't Go Breaking My Heart," a 1975 duet with Kiki Dee), anything he could wrap his enterprising little digits around. The end product was always at least as entertaining as the original, so no one was much into carping. Two of Elton's LPs, *Captain Fantastic and the Brown Dirt Cowboy* (1975) and *Rock of the Westies* (1975), became the first albums in history to enter *Billboard* at number one, the record industry's equivalent of parting the Red Sea (with Elton taking more of a Cecil B. DeMille than a Moses role).

Meanwhile, the man's wardrobe, lifestyle, and profligate spending left the meek among us dumbfounded. Elton bought mansions, private airplanes, tennis teams, amusement parks, automobile factories, multi-national oil corporations, and entire Third World countries. We don't have a precise inventory, but suffice to say, he bought oodles of trinkets. When it came to puttin' on the ritz, Elton's closet was a virtual Halloween clearing house — traces of Cher, Liberace, Jayne Mansfield, Labelle, the Rockettes, the 51st Airborne, and if you rummaged around long enough you probably would have found Mr. Blackwell himself sitting in there. Perhaps the defining image of Elton's über-man status during the mid-seventies — maybe even the defining image of the entire decade — can be found in Ken Russell's 1975 film version of *Tommy*, in which Elton played the Pinball Wizard: towering over an assembled multitude, and numbing them into submission, he was a one-man Mount Rushmore of hyperbolic meaninglessness, a glittering tabula rasa for wayward pop dreamers, and a really funny looking human being to boot.

Elton's moment came and went as unexpectedly as it flared up. Part of the problem (though not nearly as much of a factor as originally suspected) was that overstuffed closet of his ; in 1977 Elton

[1] Aka "Billie Jean, It's Not My Serve."

publicly revealed his bisexuality (surprise!), and the announcement may have cost him some public favor. Moreover, Elton didn't take to disco with the alacrity of his peers, and by the time he made a lukewarm stab at it in 1979 he'd become less newsworthy than either Robert John or Elton Motello. But the most logical explanation for Elton's sudden drop in popularity was plain and simple burnout: he did, after all, turn thirty in March 1977, coinciding almost exactly with his semi-disappearing act. He likely just looked in the mirror one day and muttered, "Enough already."

We might have muttered the same thing, and for that we now feel a twinge of regret. At a time when pop music was giddily marching itself over a cliff, Elton made sure we had lots of games 'n' stuff to keep us occupied on the way down.

Chapter 9

WE ARE WOMAN, HEAR US ROAR

"I'm trying to reach a lot of markets, and not just one. I'm not just talking about people accepting Alice Cooper, and I do not mind trying to make rock 'n' roll a real entertainment entity. Why isn't there a rock roast, such as Dean Martin and things like that?"
— Alice Cooper, 1975.

WHEN the Kinks released "Lola" in 1970, there was something eerily prescient about their return to the pop charts. Ostensibly about Ray Davies' wanton adventures at a Halloween bash, "Lola"'s key line summed up a pop moment that was barely underway: "Girls will be boys and boys will be girls/It's a mixed-up, mumbled-up, shook-up world." The moment was glam, or glitter rock, heavy metal's endearingly trashy stepsister and an early indicator that there would always be something colorful and brash to marvel over and to laugh at throughout the seventies. Glam's catwalk featured bisexual axemen, androgynous axewomen, and cross-dressing axe murderers, many of them attired in the superlative spring designs of Oscar de la Renta. Anyone who looked beyond the costumes and the hype discovered a sophisticated pop genre that ironically and irreverently pilfered hooks from fifties rock and roll, early sixties girl groups, and late sixties bubblegum. As a style, glam's roots went back to Flip Wilson, Little

Richard, Tony Curtis and Jack Lemmon in *Some Like It Hot*, Ed Wood's *Glen or Glenda*, and of course Milton Berle, who shocked American TV audiences in the 1950s with his ground-breaking gender experiments. Or maybe it all began with Oscar Wilde. Or Busby Berkeley. Or Hermaphroditus — who knows?

Whatever the case, glam rock got its start in England in the early seventies when Marc Bolan, leader of hippie-folk act Tyrannosaurus Rex, abbreviated the group's name to T. Rex, traded in his acoustic guitar for a Les Paul, and scoured his mother's wardrobe for a pair of vinyl, thigh-high boots. Between 1970 and 1973, T. Rex landed on the U.K. pop charts several times, most notably with "Hot Love" (1971), "Telegram Sam" (1972), and "Metal Guru" (1972). Their songs combined stuttered guitar phrases, gargled vocals, and lyrics that were either surreal gibberish ("Automatic Shoes, automatic shoes, give me 3-D Vision and the California blues") or pornographic gibberish ("I'm gonna s-s-s-s-s-suck ya!"). Apart from one U.S. hit in 1972 with "Bang a Gong (Get It On)," the group wasn't nearly as successful in North America, though Bolan did re-emerge a few years later as T. Rex Reed on the popular *Bang a Gong Show* .

Following T. Rex's arrival in 1970, all sorts of glam acts started flouncing their way up English pop charts, with most of them engaging in the cannibalistic ritual of decorating their faces with cake sprinkles. The biggest American success was Sweet, who began as a bubbleglam project of songwriters Nicky Chinn and Mike Chapman, and had their first U.S. hit with "Little Willy" (1973), a British version of Chuck Berry's "My Ding-A-Ling." The band decided they wanted to be taken more seriously, though ("like Blue Oyster Cult," remarked lead singer Brian Connolly), so they incorporated more of a metal sound on 1975's *Desolation Boulevard* . The LP generated classic hits in "Ballroom Blitz" (which joined the Ohio Players' "Love Rollercoaster" as the year's most thrilling amusement park rock), and "Fox on the Run," a heartfelt tribute to Fred Sanford's neverending battle with coronary thrombosis.

Sweet's arch rival on the British charts was Slade, a hand-clappin', boot-stompin' string quartet that dismayed Scrabble aficionados with a string of spectacular hits: "Gudbuy T' Jane" (1972), "Mama Weer All Crazee Now" (1972), "Cum On Feel the Noize"

(1973), and many others. True to their roots in industrial Wolverhampton, Slade upheld the highest principles of social democracy by inviting thousands of football hooligans into the studio to shout, jump, and chirp along during the making of *Slayed?* (1972), their best and most famous LP. *Slayed*'s cover even triggered a major controversy reminiscent of *Abbey Road*, as fans noticed that bassist Jimmy Lea was the only Slade person with his thumb pointing west and Band-Aids on his fingers. Much speculation ensued: Was Jimmy dead? Was he Slade's secret iconoclast? Was he nursing paper cuts?

Among England's other prominent glam stars (Mud, Roy Wood, Silverhead, Alvin Stardust, Steve 'Silk' Harley), the only ones who made it over to America were Gary Glitter, Suzi Quatro, and David Essex. Gary Glitter was actually Paul Francis Gadd, an over-the-hill performance artist who was looking for the easiest route — preferably one with a Burger King on the way — to wealth and fame. After failing to make his mark in previous eras as Danny Doo-Wop and Psammy Psychedelic, Gadd adopted the Glitter monicker, learned how to contort his face wildly whenever there was a camera in sight, and stuffed his frame into anything that looked spacey and at least three sizes too small. With "Rock and Roll Part 2" (1972), Glitter stumbled upon a worldwide smash — Americans took to its constant shouts of "Hey!" (it reminded them of Roller Derby), Burundians cheered the authentic drum tunings, Budokanese found it increased productivity when piped into the workplace, while Britons simply adored Gary's lovable mug.

Although there wasn't a need for real girls in glam — the guys took care of that department just fine — Suzi Quatro assumed the mantle anyway, becoming glam's sole female artist outside of tennis hero Renée Richards. Suzi regularly made the charts in England with such Chapmann-Chinn blockbusters as "Can the Can" (1973), "48 Crash" (1973), and "Devil's Gate Drive" (1974), but in America she made her mark as *Happy Days*' Leather Tuscadero, an alter ego to the Fonz, a menace to Mr. C., and leader of the electrifying post-glam girl group, Leather & the Suedes.

One of glitter's stranger hits was David Essex's "Rock On," a James Dean/Gene Vincent tribute that hit *Billboard* 's Top Ten in 1974. The song's swirling violins gave it an almost *noirish* ambience, which Essex later pursued in full by starring alongside the ever-mysterious Ringo in *That'll Be the Day* (1973).

With all this high-pitched delirium, it's not surprising that a couple of platformed philosophers came forth to sift through the madness, add a touch of elegance to the proceedings, and basically try to explain why everyone suddenly looked so goofy. Mott the Hoople released a series of ragged hard rock albums in the early seventies that flopped, but 1972's "All the Young Dudes," a glam slam on the Beatles and Stones, immediately established itself as glitter's acknowledged anthem and a big hit among the multitudes of gay heavy metal fans. They followed up with their best album of the decade, *Mott* (1973), after which the story got far too complex to keep track of (cf. Major Hoople's Boarding House, Motley Crüe, and Mott's Clamato Juice for more details). Roxy Music appeared on the scene with green and silver hair, an antacidic 'non-musician' named Eno (who non-played synthesizers, non-looked weird, and non-left the group in 1973), and singer Bryan Ferry, a Don Wannabe who dug art history, Bob Dylan, Lesley Gore, Humphrey Bogart, Bela Lugosi, and stamp collecting. Musically, the first five Roxy Music albums straddled between sock-hop delirium ("Editions of You," 1973, "The Thrill of It All," 1974) and erudite art rock (1974's "Song for Europe," which had French words just like the ones in Edith Piaf and Réné Simard songs), while conceptually they provided a telescopic view of Ferry's indefatigable affairs with sea nymphs, cocktail waitresses, and inflatable dolls. The group's only American hit was *Siren* 's "Love Is the Drug" (1975), a looking-for-Ms.-Goodbar adventure that left listeners to guess what happened after Ferry and his new squeeze dimmed the lights; quite likely, they just sat and stared at Bryan's glow-in-the-dark cummerbund collection.

North America didn't produce nearly as many glam acts as Britain, but one of them, Alice Cooper, made unlimited amounts of money by engaging in something called 'shock rock.' Alice's stage show was an all-ages extravaganza that included the mutilation of chickens, S&M rituals with a giant boa constrictor, mock executions of the singer himself, and, most thrilling of all, a song or two squeezed in for the musicologists in the house. About half of Alice's repertoire was as elaborate as his performances (albums veered off into morbid psychiatric confessions, gravesite romances, and sagas involving giant electric toothbrushes), but luckily he also had a gift for singles — "Eighteen" (1971), "School's Out" (1972), "Elected" (1973), "No More Mr. Nice Guy" (1973) — that sounded just fine without the visuals.

Alice's attention-getting behaviour was some sort of accomplishment when you took into account the competition he was up against on the home front. Lou Reed jumped into glam with "Walk on the Wild Side" (1972), a series of snapshots even more vivid than those in "Lola," "All the Young Dudes," or Jim Stafford's "My Girl Bill," and on 1973's *Berlin* (aka *My Son, the Folk Singer*) he set out to make glitter's definitive concept album. He missed, but *Berlin* has since influenced everything from David Bowie's *Heroes* to the Sex Pistols' "Holidays in the Sun" to Nena's "99 Luftballons." America's most colorful glitterbugs were the New York Dolls, with two albums (1973's *New York Dolls* and 1974's *In Too Much Too Soon*) that abounded in cheeky references to the Shangri-Las, old Diana Dors movies, and their Jamaican brethren the Wailers, whom they joined in bemoaning the depravity of "Babylon" (done in a "New York stylee," as lead singer David Johansen liked to boast). The least colorful was Edgar Winter, Johnny's albino brother, who reached number one in 1973 with the instrumental "Frankenstein," the same year the Dolls didn't have a hit with a non-instrumental of the same title.[1] Towards the end of 1973 Edgar and Johnny collaborated on *Winter Wonderland*, which remains a Yuletide favorite two decades later. The trend of British glam bands crossing over to America was reversed by California's Sparks, who reached number two in England with "This Town Ain't Big Enough for the Both of Us" in 1974. Although "Town" had a certain *je-ne-sais-quoi* of its own, many people saved time and money by simply adjusting the pitch on their favorite Roxy Music record to 78 RPM.

By mid-decade, glam's days were numbered. First, there was the appearance in 1975 of the Tubes (a pre-*Spinal Tap* parody act) and *The Rocky Horror Picture Show* (a pre-*Bat Out of Hell* monster flick), both of which dealt the genre a serious blow by trying to satirize

---

[1] Maybe glam actually started with Boris Karloff, who wore green face paint, a chic ornamental bolt, and big platform boots.

something that was partly conceived as satire from the outset. Next, Alice Cooper landed on *Hollywood Squares* alongside Jan Murray, Rose Marie, and Paul Lynde, where contestant after contestant took great delight in choosing "Alice to shock." Finally, glitter's most recognizable public figure had a vision one night that what the world really needed was a white version of Barry White. They called him the Jean Genie, and he was the most fun of all.

Chapter 10

Calling Occupant of Interplanetary Craft

"I get so numb. I find I'm walking around numb. I'm a bit of an iceman."
— David Bowie, 1972.

With pop music swerving off into a hundred different directions once the seventies got underway, it was only fitting that someone would construct a whole career out of recreating himself on a yearly basis and then announcing each makeover in brilliant, neon headlines. David Bowie was the rock and roll version of Sybil (portrayed by Sally Fields in a 1976 TV movie), a rubberband man of at least seventeen personalities, each one with the potential to spring forth on an unsuspecting public without warning. Alligator, Space Invader, Major Tom, Artificially-Inseminated Soul Man, and Bejewelled Pit Bull are only a handful of the Bowie personas we were treated to over the decade, and if we listed five more you'd still only be looking at the top layer of the man's costume box.

Born David Jones, but forced to change his name because record executives kept confusing him with "that guy in the Monkees," Bowie's first appearance on U.K. charts was with "Space Oddity" (1969), which successfully cashed in on the space-mania then sweeping Britain (the U.S. moon landing, reruns of *Star Trek*, hippies who 'needed their space'). He first gained attention in America for *Hunky Dory* (1971), a highly melodic outing with a vehement warning to the likes of Lennon, Jagger, and SSgt. Barry Sadler on "Changes": "Look out you rock and rollers!" "Changes" also foreshadowed the Brady Bunch's brilliant "Time To Change" from the episode where they record an ode to Peter Brady's wavering adolescent vocal chords.

Hunky Dory was well received by critics, but it was Bowie's next LP, *The Rise and Fall of Ziggy Stardust and the Spiders From Mars* (1972), that marked him as a caricature for all seasons. Here was a detached observer of a decade that piled on more excesses in its first two years than the previous decade did in ten, yet one who was as inextricably tangled up in the proceedings as Ozzy Osbourne, Helen Reddy, or any other prophet of the new age. *Ziggy Stardust* gained much notice at the time for its perplexing concept — Ziggy was an alien sent down to earth to learn a few rock and roll moves in hopes that he could one day return to his home planet as 'Zelvis' — but the album's most exciting moments were in fact provided by Mick Ronson's guitar work on "Suffragette City," "Moonage Daydream," and "Hang on to Yourself." There were also some intriguing hints of sexual awakening on David's behalf, like "the boy in the bright blue jeans" he wistfully eyes on "Lady Stardust," rumored to be Marc Bolan. Seems David wanted to "bang a gong or two" with Marc, whatever that means.

With oddball appeal working in his favor, Bowie's next move was to shock the world with a brazen series of announcements: he was bisexual and plastic (an amalgamation of Barbie and Ken), he was retiring from live performance, he had a pet goldfish named 'Zowie,' and he was about to record a concept album with some friends from the worlds of high fashion and pop — *Ziggy, Twiggy, and Iggy Sing Huey, Dewey, and Louie* . David also kept busy by producing albums for Lou Reed (*Transformer*, 1972), Mott The Hoople (*All the Young Dudes*, 1972), and the Stooges (*Raw Power*, 1973), revitalizing the careers of all three. Fans of Lou's and Iggy's recent work will now know who to thank.

Bowie's own output for the next couple years consisted of tossed-off, wigged-out, tarted-up variations on his Ziggy character.

Aladdin Sane, his first of two LPs from 1973, featured three trash classics in "Watch That Man" (crazed cannibals on the loose with utensils in hand), "Panic In Detroit" (Ché Guevara to a Diddley beat), and a cover of "Let's Spend the Night Together" (very pre-Devo). Although *Pin Ups* , Bowie's next LP, was nothing but cover versions ("Sorrow," "Friday on My Mind," and others), it did contain his hardest rock of the decade — but not, as originally promised, a set of glossies from rejected *Playgirl* and *Playboy* photo sessions.

Bowie again fell for the concept-hook on *Diamond Dogs* (1974), a pre-Bow Wow Wowie, bogus-futuristic something-or-other, complete with a tribute to George Orwell, dead 'peoploids' raised from the grave, and a spectacular glitter-guitar anthem in "Rebel Rebel." Halfway through the lavish *Diamond Dogs* tour, Bowie became wise to his own pretensions — or maybe he compared expenses with gate receipts and saw red — and scrapped the entire set. Peeling off his make-up and washing the orange food coloring out of his hair, he re-emerged as Soul Brother #157, aka the 'Thin White Duke.' This new change of costume was a resounding commercial success, as David's next two albums, *Young Americans* (1975) and *Station to Station* (1976), each yielded a major hit ("Fame" and "Golden Years," respectively). David also fulfilled a lifetime dream by becoming the first performer who closely resembled an albino to appear on *Soul Train*, where he 'hung' with Don Cornelius for a couple days and got to go shopping with Labelle.

Oddly enough, considering he was riding on the crest of so much good fortune, Bowie shifted gears again, this time ending up on the Autobahn alongside Kraftwerk (an influence), Eno (a collaborator), and Helmut Kohl (future president of West Germany, also a big fan of David's). The Berlin Trilogy (1977's *Low* and *"Heroes,"* *Lodger* from 1979) was a strange set, combining cold, synthetic textures with bits of ABBA (particularly on *Low*) and the strangest Bowie persona of all — that of an 'emotional human being.' Bowie first hinted at this transformation on "Win" from *Young Americans*, wherein he "started to feel," and by the time of *Low* he was the hardest feeling man in showbiz: weeping as he watched two young lovers separated by the Berlin Wall ("Heroes"), recoiling in horror as he pondered nuclear annihilation ("Fantastic Voyage"), agonizing endlessly over an indecent proposal to Mick Jagger ("Be My Wife"). The Berlin Wall is but a memory now, but the ghosts of David's fictional lovers can still be felt among the ruins.

Bowie was seized by another feeling in 1979, the feeling that nobody was paying much attention to him now that he was doing all this feeling, so he returned to his spaceship and headed out for parts unknown. David clones still turn up in his absence — Scary Monster, Glass Spider, Tin Machine, Suede, Luke Perry — but none have been as endearing as the original eight or nine Davids.

Chapter 11

THERE'S GOTTA BE SOME PEOPLE OUT THERE THAT LIKE TO DRINK TEQUILA

"Blue Oyster Cult is a perfect example — I LOVE THAT BAND! But there's no hero worship, no charisma. I don't wanna buy a Blue Oyster Cult lunch pail!"
— Gene Simmons, 1979.

DUKE Ellington might have seen it all coming as early as 1938, the year he composed "Prelude to a Kiss"— that the first few thousand years of man's groping existence on earth, the sum total of his follies and mishaps and embarrassments, was merely a dress rehearsal for that epochal moment in the early seventies when man's infinite capacity for making a fool of himself would erupt in the most preposterous display of runaway lunacy that human history had ever witnessed. The culprit was Kiss, a flame-shooting, tongue-lolling, patter-spouting, blood-drooling, powder-poofting pop-metal band that embodied the hapless but spirited chaos of rock music in the 1970s as well as anyone. Check your credulity at the door for a second and we'll try to explain the confluence of style and moment that made them so unique.

If you've ever glanced at a Kiss lyric sheet, it will make perfect sense that the first stop in their story is a New York grade school — P.S. 75, to be precise — where Gene Simmons began the seventies teaching elementary chemical combustion and Personal Hygiene 101 to impressionable young thumbsuckers. In his free time Gene managed to sneak away from the rarefied halls of academe to jam ravenously with musical acquaintances, a hobby that eventually led him into the nefarious clutches of Paul Stanley. The two instinctively realized they were 'meant for each other,' so they sent out an APB for a couple more like-minded bodies to bring the head count to four (the perfect configuration for a rock band, according to Gene's calculations). Recruitment ads placed in *Rolling Stone* and *The Village Voice* (after less successful attempts in *Partisan Review, The London Journal of Economics*, and *Better Homes and Gardens*) were answered by fellow New Yorkers Peter Criss and Ace Frehley, and a blubbering, slobbering, hairy behemoth began to heave itself into action. Picking a name for themselves, the guys took a private poll on their favorite sexual proclivities: "kiss" finished in a tie for fourteenth (with something called "mixed Wally flips"), but everyone agreed it had a nice ring to it anyway. To clinch the deal, the way "Kiss" rhymed with "Criss" had the power to fascinate Paul for hours.

The year was 1973, glam was queen, and our eager-beaver puckerheads knew they'd be wise to grab themselves some of this glam action before someone sounded the wake-up alarm and everyone asked for a refund. So they swiped whatever spare parts they could from the Dolls, Bowie, Slade, and anyone else who was sashaying across a rock 'n' roll runway at the time, mixed in some Arthur Brown theatrics (fire, blood, other stray bodily fluids) and plenty of infectiously simian bubblemetal guitar riffs, and then swooped in for the P.T. Barnum kill. Each member adopted a persona developed through individualized makeup, symbolic iconography, and enigmatic press bios that knew neither modesty nor sanity: Paul declared himself starry-eyed Love God of the entire universe, even more virile and insatiable than Don Knotts; Gene mutated into a hulking S&M cenobite, complete with an acrobatic tongue and a partly triangulated, partly bobbed haircut that defied description; Ace revealed he was from another planet altogether, although none of our eight neighbors was in any hurry to claim responsibility; and Peter dressed up like a roly-poly tomcat, and no, nobody understood why. They briefly considered adding a construction worker and an Indian

Chief to the roster, but we'll pick up that particular ball and run with it later in the book.

Over the next two years, Kiss released three albums in quick succession: *Kiss* ("I like it," nodded Ace approvingly, "it's a title that makes you think of us") and *Hotter Than Hell* , both from 1974, and *Dressed To Kill* in 1975. All sold well, and each one had a few signature Kiss tunes. In many, like "Deuce," "Strutter," "Hotter Than Hell," and "Room Service," the band laid out their rigorously constructed views on sexual roles and mores in the post-liberated age. In "Cold Gin," "Rock Bottom," and "Black Diamond," they cast a keen sociologist's eye over the seamier side of prolonged urban blight; and in "Let Me Go, Rock 'N Roll" and "Rock and Roll All Nite" they blew party horns, danced the jitterbug, and wore lampshades.

Kiss toured frantically during their early years, so much so that they boldly plunged ahead with a double-live LP. It was a move that paid off spectacularly: *Alive!* (1975) remains an essential seventies record, at once a nonstop glitter rave-up, a complex doorway to an entire industry metamorphosing into a joke, and an unparalleled goldmine for scholars of motormouth stage patter. The LP made Kiss bonafide American heroes just in time for the Bicentennial; "Yes," you could almost hear the founding fathers sigh from above, "the country is in good hands."

Nineteen seventy-six proved to be Kiss's biggest year by far: a best-selling poster that captured the band in revolutionary pose (as if Ace's spacesuit costume wasn't enough of a rallying inspiration to millions), a Top Ten single ("Beth," a rare glimpse into the vulnerability that Peter kept hidden away behind his whiskers), stadium sellouts everywhere, and the release of their fourth and best studio LP, *Destroyer*. Alongside a couple more all-time Kiss hootenannies in "Shout It Out Loud" and "Detroit Rock City," *Destroyer* took a conceptual journey deep into the psyche of each member, laying bare the hopes, dreams, and doubts that followed the guys home after the amps were turned off and the smoke cleared. No private anguish was left undocumented: "You like my seven-inch leather heels," mused Paul wistfully, "and goin' to all of the shows/BUT/Do you love me?" It was just like the Shirelles.

Although Kiss never again matched their *Alive!*/*Destroyer* peak on the goosebump meter, their popularity didn't wane a bit for the rest of the decade. *Rock and Roll Over* (1976) more or less did (smelled just like a mangy old dog, said many), but 1977's *Love Gun* was an energetic return to form, highlighted by "Christine Sixteen," another you-take-the-kids-to-the-movie-honey-and-I'll-stay-home-with-the-babysitter love ballad of the kind Kiss specialized in. They finished the year with Paul reading somewhere that once a human brain cell is dead, it's never again replaced. "Hey, get a load of this," he called over to the others, and a couple of weeks later *Alive II* was released to thundering approval from fans.

Meanwhile, the band had begun to branch out. First, there was the formation of the Kiss Army: for $5.00, kids could enlist in a clandestine organization that flew secret reconnaissance missions into Communist Bloc countries and captured fertile young maidens by the hundreds. Second came a Kiss comic book produced by Marvel Comics, which sold nearly half-a-million copies during the summer of 1977. (A Kiss comic book being somewhat redundant, everyone in the band started carrying around an official ID card certifying him as 'the real person' to avoid any confusion with his cartoon alter ego.)

Things got really weird in 1978: NBC aired a made-for-TV movie, *Kiss Meets the Phantom of the Park* ("In the great tradition of *Brian's Song* and *Roots*," went NBC's promo), and then all four members followed with simultaneous solo albums (a trio LP, *The Golden Hits of Peter, Paul & Ace*, was recorded but never released). By 1979 Kiss was functioning as a group again, and they said goodbye to the decade in the best of all possible ways with a huge disco hit, "I Was Made For Lovin' You." The most improbable of all their classic singles, "Lovin' You" was ingenious testament to the band's commercial savvy, stylistic flexibility, and COMPLETE AND UTTER LACK OF CONVICTION ABOUT ANYTHING IN THEIR ENTIRE LIVES. They were truly something to behold.

You still can (behold them, that is), but it's not the same. Peter's long gone, Ace is long gone, the Kiss Army's long gone, the makeup's long gone,[1] and the magic's long gone. Don Knotts and P.S.

---

[1] Discarded with much fanfare in the early eighties; the moment it was removed, innocent bystanders pleaded with them to relinquish their instruments instead.

75 are still standing, but for how much longer is anybody's guess. The Kiss that slogs away in 1993 — Gene, Paul, and whoever else they're paying these days to help keep the stage level — is just one among many pointless heavy metal bands. They used to be the *most* pointless, however, and they used to make a celebration of their pointlessness. That made all the difference in the seventies.

Chapter 12

GUESS WHO'S COMING TO DINNER?

"Basically, we just like to sort of get out and rock and roll for the people 'cause that's what rock and roll is all about, so in that sense there's no real pressure to put anything over on anybody."
— Rod Price of Foghat, 1976.

EVERYONE understands what heavy metal and glam were, but there was a third kind of guitar rock in the early-to-mid-seventies that flourished in reaction to the other two and captured as vividly as anything the tenor of the times. It had no specific name, and to a certain extent it was an amorphous dumping ground for whatever 4/4 rock and roll couldn't be defined as heavy metal or glam, but it must have been real because we know instinctively who belongs there, and we even have a name for it: Hard Rockin' Shit, henceforth abbreviated to HRS. You've probably seen a barrage of HRS commercials on television recently, pitches for compilation albums like *Guitar Anthems*, *Guitar Monsters*, *Monster Guitar Anthems*, *Hard Rockin' Guitars*, *Anthemic and Monstrously Hard Guitar Rock*, and even more creative permutations. There's rarely any heavy metal proper on these collections, no Led Zeppelin or Black Sabbath or Deep Purple, because heavy metal was decadent, evil, and disrespected the blues; no glam, because the only cross-dressing that Mountain's Leslie West approved of involved mixing Thousand Islands and French and Blue Cheese in a big vat of chef's salad and slurping it all up; no zydeco, because really, how monstrous can an accordion riff be? That was the underlying paradox of HRS: rather than ranting against James Taylor or Seals & Crofts, its deepest contempt was reserved for anything that smacked of sensationalism or exploitation, meaning exactly those people — Elton, the Dolls, Kiss, Mott the Hoople, the Stooges — who were in fact responsible for the liveliest and most enduring hard rock of the era.

In lieu of brazenly crass hi-jinks, HRS recruits operated under an unwavering respect for a few humble precepts:

1) Give the impression that your sole purpose in life is to churn out the one or two Chuck Berry riffs you've mastered.

2) When interviewed, constantly jabber on about your 'no frills' approach to rock and roll, or how 'heavy,' 'tight,' or 'together' your band is.

3) However adamantly you're opposed to gimmickry, make sure you appropriate just enough — dry ice, ridiculous posturing, and double-live — to make a living.

4) Always look like you'd be more at home on a loading dock than in the pages of *Creem* — denim, beards, rotundity, it all helps.

5) When the Berry riffs run out, come clean and admit you have no purpose in life. People will forgive, and remember you with love.

Well, we do remember, and we do forgive; in its own cloddish way, HRS produced more than a few inexplicable miracles. A couple of the best, Mountain's "Mississippi Queen" and Free's "All Right Now," lumbered forth just as the decade began. Probably no two songs in rock history have inspired as much ritualistic grunting among males between the ages of fourteen and twenty-five. Mountain was a Cream-modelled 'power trio' from New York led by the aforementioned Leslie West, 'West' being something of a misnomer since his staggering frame also covered ample territory in the east, north, and south. Free came from Britain, where "All Right Now" reached number two on singles charts — what Winston Churchill would have looked like in Sumo wrestling garb, that's what "All Right Now" sounded like.

Another early touchstone was the *Allman Brothers Band at Fillmore East* (1971), which at seven songs spread over four sides averaged out to hardly any songs per side. Although the Allmans' "Ramblin Man" (1973) would later help invent Southern Rock, an HRS subgenre that peaked in the middle of the decade, it was with *Fillmore East* that they truly made HRS history: reverential twenty-minute blues jams, lots of talk about 'mamas' and 'the road,' and a gatefold cover replete with beer cans, roadies, and towering crates of touring equipment. (Loyal fans of the album are advised to keep reading, because very shortly we'll be getting to the Osmond Brothers, the Cassidy Brothers, and the future Mrs. Cher Allman.)

Right from the start, HRS attached profound spiritual significance to a human transaction called 'boogie.' Few of us really know what the word means, and some of us don't even like to say it, but familiarity with its intricacies was part of an HRS zealot's basic training. Britain's Humble Pie, in particular, got up and boogied, got down and woogied, flipped over and oogied, and if we have to blame someone for the ensuing boogie madness that swept through the decade, let's blame them. *Performance: Rockin' the Fillmore* (1971) was Pie's big HRS statement, four sides, seven songs, and lots of blues covers which should not be confused with any Allman Brothers record of vaguely similar title, style, and configuration. The Allmans were merely *at* the Fillmore, while the Pie was in an adjacent wing *rockin'* the Fillmore.

Foghat, another British band, plodded where few dared to plod, and pummeled as few knew how to pummel. Their album titles say it all: *Foghat* (1972), *Foghat Rock and Roll* (1973), *Rock and Roll Outlaws* (1974), and the highly offbeat *Outlaw Foghat* (1975). Leading the American boogie charge were Atlanta's Little Feat ("Triple Face Boogie," 1974) and Boston's J. Geils Band (featuring a white harmonica player with a three-ton afro), both of whom boogied and boogied until the very life force was sucked out through their eye sockets and spread to the four corners of the earth. Later, of course, came Doogie Howser.

Returning to the sloth-footed brontosauri-riffuramulus genus, Nazareth was the meanest, rockingest Scottish export during the barren days between the Royal Scots Dragoon Guards and the Bay City Rollers. In addition to the controversy generated by their audaciously sacrilegious name, Nazareth also gained attention because of some surprisingly folky sources for cover material: the Everly Brothers'

"Love Hurts" (1975), Joni Mitchell's "This Flight Tonight" (1973), Crazy Horse's "Gone Dead Train" (1978), Slim Whitman's "Hair of the Dog" (1975), Boxcar Willie's "My White Bicycle" (1975), oddities like that. Equally 'down' and 'dirty' was England's Bad Company, who came along in the mid-seventies to land two singles in the Top Ten, "Can't Get Enough" in 1974 and "Feel Like Makin' Love" a year later. "Naturally we dug Barry White's *Can't Get Enough* and Roberta Flack's 'Feel Like Makin' Love,'" explained Paul Rodgers, "but the whole thing had gotten out of hand — we wanted a tighter kind of sound, no frills." New York's Foreigner, an American version of Bad Company, weren't nearly so sure of themselves — in the space of a year they charted with "Cold As Ice" (1977) and "Hot Blooded" (1978), eventually finding a happy medium on their autobiographical *Room Temperature* LP (1979). Passing mention must also be made of Argent, a collection of resurrected Zombies whose only American hit, "Hold Your Head Up," made the Top Ten in 1972. Few who witnessed it will forget the sight of Rod Argent in concert, assailing his Hammond organ mercilessly while imploring everyone to "HOLD YOUR HEAD UP! HOLD YOUR HEAD UP!", followed by that magical moment when a good third of his audience would summon the willpower to do exactly that.

Although 'paying one's dues' and being a 'survivor' were paramount in the HRS cosmology, all it really took to ensure HRS immortality was one certified Bigfoot anthem. Brownsville Station's "Smokin' in the Boy's Room" (1973) was as punky as HRS ever got, and one of the decade's true revolutionary assaults on the education system along with Alice's "School's Out," Tull's "Teacher," Supertramp's "Bloody Well Right," and John Sebastian's "Welcome Back." Rick Derringer, already a fabled figure for his participation on the McCoys' "Hang on Sloopy," found the HRS motherlode in 1974 with "Rock and Roll, Hoochie Koo," still a popular line dance nearly twenty years later. (The phrase 'hoochie koo,' should anyone be interested, was derived from Hu Shi Ku II, emperor of Japan during the fifth Ming Dynasty.) And then there was Joe Walsh, who found time between the James Gang and the Eagles to belch out "Rocky Mountain Way" (1973), a song which had something to do with John Denver, apparently, and was sung through a megaphone.

It's difficult to pinpoint a guiding moral force within the HRS hierarchy — true exemplars led by deed and not by word — but you couldn't do better than a couple of fraternal Canadian bands, the Guess Who and Bachman-Turner Overdrive. The Guess Who was a true conundrum. On the one hand they were as poppy as could be, with an extended run of hit singles in the early seventies, but at the same time they were fronted by one of the grouchiest of seventies rock stars, Burton Cummings — a bitter naysayer, dour gadfly, and cynical prophet of doom who didn't have a good word to say about hippies, 9 to 5 commuters, real females, pretend females, or anyone else except Wolfman Jack. The Guess Who's greatest moment was "American Woman" (1970), one of the decade's three indisputable *Wayne's World* riff-orgies ("Whole Lotta Love" and Bill Conti's "Gonna Fly Now" being the others), and with "Glamour Boy" (1973) Burton articulated the growing dismay of the HRS generation: "Forty-nine thousand dollars, you can look like a woman tonight/Forty-nine thousand dollars, I think it'll work out right." The New York Dolls, among others, found themselves deeply shamed by this all-out ambush.

Bachman-Turner Overdrive was led by Randy Bachman, who began the 1970s as a guitarist for the Guess Who. When his former mates started to fade in 1974, BTO seized the moment and became Canada's HRS ambassadors to the world. There was a certain recklessness about BTO, a headstrong volatility in the face of harsh Manitoban winters and omnipresent wheat droughts, that consumed such unforgettable Prairie stomps as "Takin' Care of Business" (1974), "You Ain't Seen Nothin' Yet" (1974), "Roll on Down the Highway" (1975), and "Hey You" (1975) in intoxicating, tractor-trailer-sized hauls of unbridled blue-collar joy. They rolled and they rolled and they rolled, and when the highway finally ran out of road they pulled into the first donut shop they saw, sat themselves down for a big long spell, and commenced to 'take care of business.'

Another key HRS band to emerge in the mid-seventies was Lynyrd Skynyrd, an extended family of axe-happy Bubbas and Bubbettes from the murky swamplands and hazardous mini-putt golf courses of coastal Florida. Guitars were Skynyrd's trademark: not just the traditional lead-rhythm arrangement but three, four, five guitars at a time, a cascading phalanx of low-slung assault weaponry, a perfectly synchronized mass of ascending and descending scales, enough guitars to choke an antelope or two. Their breakthrough hit came in 1974 with "Sweet Home Alabama," a scathing indictment of a certain holier-than-thou singer-songwriter who had lately begun to betray his deep Southern gospel roots: "Well I hope Neil Diamond will remember/Brother Love don't need him around, anyhow!" As time passed Skynyrd became most identified with "Free Bird" (1974), which was picked up by AOR radio and turned into the number-one rival to "Stairway to Heaven" and "Layla" as the unofficial mantra for a lost generation of teenage Alfred E. Newmans. But unlike the soaring bird they celebrated, Skynyrd and the friendly skies were not particularly compatible: a 1977 plane crash killed singer Ronnie Van Zandt and two other members, cutting the band down in its prime.

By this time Skynyrd had ushered in a Southern Rock insurrection. *Hee Haw* was a big part of it, as was Burt Reynolds' brilliant cycle of Gator films, but at its heart and soul was some of the rudest, gnarliest, rebel-rousingest HRS this side of the Oak Tree Boys. It was one big Dixie hoedown, as band after band of long-haired Jethro Bodines upped the ampage, unfurled their Confederate flags, and played ghost-ridin' hoodoo chants deep into the night. The best non-Skynyrd song to emerge from the maelstrom was "Tush" (1973) by ZZ Top, three ten-gallon yahoos from Texas with indescribably funny beards.

The South's orneriest cheerleaders were the Charlie Daniels Band, who on hits like "The South's Gonna Do It" (1975) and "The Devil Went Down to Georgia" (1979) pined for "truck stop breakfasts, late-night poker games, and early morning hangovers." Charlie had a beard too, though his was more of the Ronnie Hawkins/Burl Ives variety. The Outlaws, a Floridian rival of Skynyrd's, had a colossal-sized AOR anthem with "Green Grass and High Tides" (1975), and more guitars than Skynyrd, Les Paul, and Tex & Edna's Factory Music Outlet put together — they add a new one every year, and at last count were up to thirty-one. The Marshall Tucker Band ("Heard It in a Love Song," 1977), Atlanta Rhythm Section ("So Into You," 1977), and Elvin Bishop ("Fooled Around and Fell in Love," 1976) also hit nationally, as Southern Rock asserted itself as HRS's truest stronghold in the waning days before punk and disco.

For heroically carrying a flag that didn't need to be carried, and for carrying it in the wrong direction, we hereby salute the Hard Rockin' Shit of our youth — that mysterious gray area between heavy metal and Grizzly Adams, the place where pomp, circumstance, and party barrels of Kentucky Fried Chicken went to die. Sadly we never got to give Black Oak Arkansas ("Jim Dandy," 1973), the Ozark Mountain Daredevils ("If You Wanna Get to Heaven," 1974), Status Quo ("Rockin' All Over the World," 1975), Thin Lizzy ("The Boys Are Back in Town," 1976), Trooper ("Raise a Little Hell," 1978), or a hundred other worthy foot soldiers their due, but it's time to shift gears. Glam, heavy metal, and Bette Midler's scurrilous "Boogie Woogie Bugle Boy" (1973) weren't the only things causing grief for the guys in Foghat. Join us, as we go for a midnight swim in topographic oceans.

Chapter 13

A FIFTH OF RACHMANINOFF

"Copland heard my arrangement of 'Hoedown' and he was knocked out by it. The only thing he said was why hadn't I played the triplets in a certain bar. We'd altered it with a very finely dotted quaver because it didn't swing the other way."
— Keith Emerson, 1977.

GIVEN rock and roll's immense role in our daily lives, the way we look to Ice-T and Firehouse for moral direction and spiritual leadership, it's hard to believe there was a time when the music was not considered art, when it was heresy to mention Elvis or the Kingsmen in the same breath as Mozart, Wordsworth, or Godzilla movies. That was pretty much the case until the mid-sixties, however, when attitudes began to shift and teenage music became accepted as one of the twentieth century's key artistic movements. First, there was the arrival in 1965 of Simon & Garfunkel, the latter of whom was often referred to as "Arty." A year later, the Rolling Stones and Gary Lewis & the Playboys introduced the word 'paint' into rock's vocabulary ("Paint It Black" and "You Don't Have to Paint Me a Picture," respectively). Finally, Mason Williams released "Classical Gas" in 1968, inspiring legions of rock and non-rock fans alike to join in the refrain, "Classical gas/It's a gas, gas, gas." Clearly a new kind of music was coming into being, a highbrow pop tradition that would flourish in the seventies under the name "art rock," dwarfing along the way even heavy metal and glam in terms of abject human debasement and tragically inflated ambition. This modern day Tower of Babel was quickly dubbed "progressive rock" by enthusiasts, a phrase that remains as puzzling a non sequitur as "political integrity" or "Frampton Comes Alive."

If, in days of future passed, art rock will be remembered for anything, it will most likely be for its utilization of the synthesizer, an electronic keyboard developed for popular usage by Rev. Sun Myung Moog in 1968. The synthesizer was the first instrument (Yoko Ono excepted) that could effectively mimic the sounds of an orchestra, a grandfather clock, or a buzzing lear jet, and its unique palette of noises zabodjulated and whoogoozied listeners into helpless, numbed submission. A select group of synth–heroes became closely identified with this wonderful new hardware: German über-groups Kraftwerk and Tangerine Dream, balding non-Aryans Brian Eno and Terry Riley, France's Jean-Michel Jarré, and the always delightful Synergy. The Dream in particular were such uncompromising electronic purists, they even made it a point of honor to inscribe "no acoustic instruments whatsoever used in this recording" on the back of their remarkable *Alpha Centauri* LP (1971).

Any discussion of art rock has to begin with Pink Floyd, especially since we're saving Pink Lady for later in the book. Originally part of the late-sixties British response to American psychedelia (an august collection of bands that included the Nice, Tomorrow, the Status Quo, the Mixed-Up World of Arthur Brown, the Purple Milk Crates, and Antelope Snuff), Floyd made their first big statement of the seventies on *Meddle* (1971). The album is still beloved for its side-long composition "Echoes," twenty minutes of the entire band shouting "Hello, down there" inside the Grand Canyon. Next came their monumental commercial breakthrough, *The Dark Side of the Moon* (1973), an intricately philosophical song cycle about time, death, madness, and the bad lifestyle habits of famous drummers. In many ways, the LP was similar to Wishbone Ash's *Argus* (1972), although Floyd seemed to shy away from the more mythical implications of contemporary malaise that haunted the Wishbones. *Moon*'s array of production techniques and everyday sound effects — helicopters, heartbeats, cash registers, laughing hyenas supplied by Joan Embry of the San Diego Zoo — was overwhelming; just thinking about "On the Run," where the music passes back and forth between speakers really fast, brings back vivid five-dimensional flashbacks.

After two more gargantuan releases (1975's *Wish You Were Here* , 1977's *Animals*) and suitably outlandish tours (complete with flying pigs, exploding airplanes, and private tarot card readings for all in attendance), Floyd closed out the decade with the grand finale of seventies concept albums, *The Wall* (1979). Among other things, the album generated a number-one single ("Another Brick in the Wall"), an animated movie, a Berlin Wall benefit performance, a TV sitcom (*Three Bricks Shy of a Load*), a tribute band (Wall of Voodoo), and a franchise of furniture outlets (the Brick).

The only art rock band that has outlived Pink Floyd is Genesis, who began the seventies under the direction of Peter Gabriel. This first phase produced unforgettable fables like "Return of the Giant Hogweed" (a 1971 sequel to "Look, Here Comes a Giant Hogweed"), "Supper's Ready" (1972), and "Firth of Frith" (1973); all were essential companions to J.R.R. Tolkien's *The Hobbit* and T.S. Geisel's *The Cat In the Hat* . The Gabriel years climaxed with *The Lamb Lies Down on Broadway* (1974), a double-set matched only by the Old Testament in scope, revelation, sheer physical weight, and compelling characters (Rael, some carpet crawlers, a porcupine, a fly, a colony of slippermen, and — our favorite —'it'). Much of the album was unusually poppy, so some may prefer the wordless reggae-dub version, *Silence of the Lamb* (1975). When Gabriel left the group in 1975, he handed over the reins to drummer Phil Collins; Genesis remains busy inventing crazy new dance steps even as we write.

Pink Floyd and Genesis stood out as musical minimalists next to Yes, Jethro Tull, and Emerson, Lake & Palmer, three classically-oriented groups that never failed to spice up their albums with an eighteen-piece flugel horn brigade, a twenty minute Prokofiev coda performed on spoons, or a sudden time signature change from 3/4 to 17.5/6.7, just to mix things up a bit.

Yes was the most accessible of the three, thanks to the guitar work of Steve Howe and the Byrdsy, quadruple-tracked vocals of Jon Anderson (one of art rock's great chameleons, taking a run at the U.S.

Presidency in 1980 and then launching a successful country & western career thereafter). Two of Yes's early compositions, "I've Seen All Good People" (1971) and "Roundabout" (1972), were true seventies classics, exhibiting a musical sophistication and intellectual prowess that left Three Dog Night and Bobby Sherman fans dumbfounded. Between 1973 and 1974 Yes really got untracked, releasing a triple-live album (*Yessongs*, 1973), a four-sided, four-song opus (*Tales from Topographic Oceans*, 1973), and a three-song suite (*Relayer*, 1974). Each was an open-ended stopover in a seamless transcendental journey, a prismatic mirror reflecting life's deepest mysteries. Also of interest, keyboardist Rick Wakeman was the inspiration for the ill-fated "Sony Wakeman," a special Japanese synthesizer that subway commuters could strap around their heads to drown out the monotonous din of everyday life.

Jethro Tull was fronted by Ian Anderson, a pied pipin', elfishly bug-eyed prodigy who had a soft spot for Arthurian legends and cross-dressing minstrels. *Aqualung* (1971) was Tull's first major work of the seventies, a morality play about organized religion and decrepit old men which featured a couple of prime air-flute monsters in the title track and "Locomotive Breath." Although "Living in the Past" (1972) and "Bungle in the Jungle" (1974) almost reached the Top Ten, hit singles were accidental blips in the Tull universe. The real fun took place on *Thick As a Brick* (1972) and *A Passion Play* (1973), one-song LPs that came with opera glasses, ballet slippers, and wind-up music boxes to ensure that there wouldn't be any dead spots while you flipped the record over. By the middle of the decade Tull began to keep a lower profile, sequestering themselves in a private world where the village was green, the water was pure, and the trolls were frisky.

Emerson, Lake & Palmer was a British supergroup made up of former Nice, King Crimson, and Atomic Rooster members.[1] The main attraction of ELP's self-titled debut album (1971) was "Lucky Man," a Greg Lake ballad with Moog pyrotechnics that remain unsurpassed in transonic imagery and high-decibel clarity. Most of ELP's subsequent output consisted of exhausting keyboard drills like "Karn Evil 9,"

---

[1] Bill Haley was originally slated to be part of the lineup, but was given his walking papers when it was discovered that the acronym HELP would play right into the hands of rock critics everywhere.

which came in three movements (up, down, sideways) and was the centrepiece of the band's all-you-can-eat masterwork, *Brain Salad Surgery* (1973). They were also fond of reworking the classics (Moussorgsky's "Pictures at an Exhibition," Aaron Copland's "Fanfare for the Common Man," Sir Robert Nevil's "C'est La Vie," many others), providing an enlightening education for provincial dullards who didn't know Monteverdi from Mantovani, Walter Carlos from Wendy Carlos, or Vaughn Williams from Anson Williams.

While all of the aforementioned groups landed a hit single or two in the seventies, art rock was also home to a few maestros and impresarios who consistently made their biggest strides in the Top Forty arena, confounding all scholarly distinctions between music that made you smart and music that left you as dumb as a chair. The best and brightest of the art-pop bands was the Electric Light Orchestra, an offshoot of British cult favorites the Move ("Do Ya" and "California Man," 1972). Under the guidance of Jeff Lynne, ELO travelled a path that was the reverse of their art rock contemporaries: early albums had overtures, choirs, and densely layered symphonic wheezing; *New World Record* (1976) sounded like the second coming of *Abbey Road*; by 1979, everyone confused them with ABBA. It was a startling transformation that began with "Can't Get It Out of My Head" (1975) and never let up for the rest of the decade. Some highlights: "Evil Woman" (1975), rumored to be about either Carly Simon or David Bowie, was anchored by a piano riff that helped invent house music; "Telephone Line" (1977) placed a conference call to Jim Croce ("Operator"), Dr. Hook ("Sylvia's Mother"), Sugarloaf ("Don't Call Us, We'll Call You"), and the Sylvers ("Hot Line"); and "Don't Bring Me Down" (1979) roundly condemned the negativity of Joe Jackson and other punk rock depressives. As final proof of ELO's stature, Randy Newman wrote a song about them ("The Story of a Rock and Roll Band"). This puts them in a league with Lester Maddox, Sigmund Freud, and God.

Another AM mainstay throughout the decade was Queen, a travelling theatre-in-the-round troupe where art rock met glam, metal commingled with *La Boheme* , orthodoxy gave way to orthodontics, and Charles Darwin's theories were continually brought into question. Singer Freddie Mercury was the group's major attraction, and certainly there were few pop stars in the seventies who could match his wry, extravagant, pan-sexual sense of human tragedy: "Life is a cabaret," Freddie's every gesture seemed to sigh, "I wanna ride it all night long." Musically Queen was all over the place, dabbling in opera ("Somebody to Love," 1976), Steam-like hockey chants ("We Will Rock You," 1977), exciting hillbilly simulations ("Crazy Little Thing Called Love," 1979), and whatever else satisfied Freddie's insatiable appetite for adventure. Their summit achievement, "Bohemian Rhapsody" (1976), has inspired one generation of teenagers after another to bob rhythmically during the metal part and gesticulate wildly during the Italian part.[2]

Art Rock had its own social and political agenda, too, a frontline engagement that was vigilantly pursued by Supertramp. In naming 'Tramp's *Even in the Quietest Moments* (1979) his favorite LP ever, writer Ritchie Yorke movingly captured their unique appeal: "Supertramp are the worthy inheritors of rock's grand idealism as manifested in assorted music of the late sixties. Unlike most of their contemporaries, Supertramp are obviously not afraid to lash out at the complacency of the seventies..." And lash out they did, taking on educators ("School" and "Bloody Well Right" from 1974's *Crime of the Century*), the salmon-fishing lobby ("Downstream," 1977), Denny's Restaurants (*Breakfast in America* , 1979), and many other formless, invidious villains. It also bears mentioning that Supertramp was notorious for fussing endlessly over their tour sound system: soundchecks sometimes lasted weeks, and after every show audience members were asked to rate low, mid, and high range frequencies.

The U.K. produced a number of other bands that helped to make art rock the wondrous thing it was throughout the seventies. The Moody Blues fired up their mellotrons for "Question" (1970), "The Story in Your Eyes" (1971), and the resurrected "Nights in White Satin" (1972), and they also demonstrated a keen awareness of professional golf on "Isn't Curtis Strange?" (1972). The jocular guitar hijinks of Robert Fripp turned King Crimson into a fan favorite, with *Lark's Tongue in Aspic* (1973) and *Starless and Bible Black* (1974)

[2.] Unlike most rock fans, we do not subscibe to the theory that Freddie Mercury died in 1991 — the appearance of Right Said Freddie's "I'm Too Sexy" only months later was just too coincidental.

opening up unexplored territory that neither of Robert's post-Crimson projects, 'Frippertronics' or 'Gladys Knight & the Fripps,' got anywhere near. Mike Oldfield's *Tubular Bells* (1973) provided the theme music for *The Exorcist*, one of the decade's landmark scare films, but when he tried to duplicate the feat on 1977's *Baroque Variations on a Theme Suggested by Piranha,* he found himself on much shakier ground. Speaking of great titles, Gentle Giant's *Pretentious* (1977) was one of the best, almost as incisive as Van Der Graaf Generator's *H to He Who Am the Only One* (1970) or Gong's *Gazeuse* (1977). You probably already know about not feeding stray gazeuses — they just can't be trusted.

Although art rock did not breed nearly as rapidly on North American soil, there was nonetheless a handful of practitioners that managed to explore the deepest dungeons and tame the wildest dragons. Chicago's Styx made their presence felt time and time again with stately ballads ("Come Sail Away,"1977; "Babe," 1979) and raging wind tunnels ("Lady," 1975; "Lorelei," 1976), and when they bid us "Welcome to the Grand Illusion" in 1977, it was obvious they felt betrayed by the shallowness that engulfed them, the refusal of Prism, Saga, Alan Parsons, and their other peers to confront the 1970s in any meaningful way. A complex band, they were perhaps best summed up by A&M's ingenious ad campaign: "Pick up Styx."

Kansas mined a similarly contemplative vein, first giving fatherly advice on "Carry on Wayward Son" (1976), then later returning to the days of Steinbeck, Guthrie, and displaced migrant farmers on "Dust in the Wind" (1978). Todd Rundgren tried his hand at many things in the seventies — singer-songwriter (*Something/Anything*, 1972), glam (*Todd*, 1973), Klaatu cover band (*Faithful*, 1976) — but he was more or less an art rocker at heart, an obsessive mixing-board pedant with cyberactive nerve endings and sallow bone structure. Gradually, Todd devoted more and more of his energies to a side project called Utopia ('the Shangri-Las' had already been taken), barricading himself deeper and deeper in a cosmic hologram of his own making. Perhaps he caught a glimpse of Starcastle in there, creators of the sadly neglected *Citadel* (1977). Those who seek knowledge, seek Starcastle; if it's just burgers you're after, any old White Castle will do.

For over two decades, art rock has survived in the face of

critical scorn, public ridicule, Apollo 100's "Joy", Deodato's "Also Sprach Zarathustra", Walter Murphy's "A Fifth of Beethoven", Bram Tchaikovsky, *Hooked on Classics*, Falco's "Rock Me Amadeus," Sebastian Bach, and many other assaults on its organic structure too numerous to catalogue. Thanks to the revitalizing efforts of Marillion, Gowan, King's X, Faith No More, and Andreas Vollenweider, we can still go back to the source and learn something new. Floyd, ELP, Crimson, Gong — they turned pop music inside out 'til it ended up being twelve times as large, slowly making its way through thickets of hogweeds to an unknown destination.

Chapter 14

THIS USED TO BE CLINT'S PLAYGROUND: THE DYNAMIC, EXPLOSIVE, SUPER BAD WORLD OF K-TEL RECORDS

"The consumer must receive value for money. That is the first truth of the music business — of any business."
— K-Tel International's Gary Kieves.

THE chasm that was created by *Sgt. Pepper* in 1967 — separating 'pop' from 'rock,' 'frivolous' from 'serious,' 'fake' from 'real,' and 'Peaches' from 'Herb' — became even more pronounced in the early seventies. On one side were art-rockers, singer-songwriters, HRS galumphs, and whoever else took pride in belonging to the great Pete Seeger/Frank Zappa/Rod McKuen tradition of quality, serious- ness, and musicianship; on the other side was the slime pit, where the only thing that mattered was money, money, and number-one singles. The pit was a unique and troubling place — a murky, dank, frightening netherworld of Polka Rock, Martial-Arts Rock, and million- selling singles by nuns, Swedes, truckers, and popcorn machines. It was ruled by a company called K-Tel International. It made no sense then, it makes even less sense now.

Inside the pit, the music played and the kids danced while a frantic voice issued non-stop bulletins: "That's Right 24 Original Hits

By 24 Original Artists You'd Pay Over $43.50 If You Bought These Songs Separately You'd Also Be Clinically Insane Please Call Now Operators Are Standing By I'm Out Of Breath Help —" It was the voice of K-Tel International, a Canadian-based record label that licensed the tackiest, strangest, and crassest Top Forty hits of the day from bigger record labels, crammed as many of them as possible into garishly packaged compilation albums bearing the crudest titles imaginable, and then pedalled the finished product via hyperdriven TV commercials that made the records themselves seem modest by comparison.

K-Tel's roots go back to Western Canada in the mid-sixties, where Philip and Raymond Kieves came up with the idea of marketing a record album called *24 Goofy Greats* (1966) directly over TV. As this was the first time in recorded history that the Aristotelian ideals of 'goofy' and 'great' had been so closely linked, curious citizens flocked to their telephones and ordered up a storm. *24 Goofy Greats* was about as tasteful as K-Tel ever got, and by the early seventies its expanding roster of titles began to suggest the onset of dementia: *Block Buster, Dynamite, 22 Explosive Hits, Super Bad, Kooky Toones, Polka Voodoo, Whammo Blammo, Psycho Wing-Dings, The Best of Eddy Arnold,* there seemed no limit to the madness. Album jackets featured swirling colors, violent starbursts, ridiculously oversized lettering, and the ubiquitous "as advertised on TV" bubble that was the K-Tel equivalent of the toxic skeleton symbol. For hardcore K-Tel collectors, there were ordering instructions on the back cover for the 'Record Selector,' a "space age device for storing and selecting your records."[1] Once you'd been mesmerized by the commercials, received your album in the mail, filed it in the Record Selector, retrieved it from the Record Selector, fully absorbed the packaging, and placed it on your turntable, all that remained was to curl up into a little ball and marvel at the music. Come and hitch a ride with us, then, as we embark on a roughly chronological tour through the K-Tel compost heap.

Bizarre hit singles started popping up everywhere in 1970, and bizarre was where K-Tel did its recruiting. Mungo Jerry's "In The Summertime" and Norman Greenbaum's "Spirit in the Sky" were early K-Tel archetypes: brash, quirky, exuberant, preposterous, and easy to

---

[1] Much to K-Tel's credit, the original blueprints for the Record Selector would later play an important role in the development of the space shuttle.

chop up into three-second snippets for TV. One of the hallmarks of K-Tel right from the start was its trailblazing commitment to the pan-global World Beat sound, so you could always count on the inclusion of foreign intrigues like the Shocking Blue's "Venus" and the Tee Set's "Ma Belle Amie," two Dutch bands that unclogged your synapses and gently rotated the windmills of your mind. Straight outta Pittsburgh came the Jaggerz with "The Rapper," a dope (i.e., incredibly stupid) gangster epic by a band whose name terrified many — wasn't one Jagger enough already? No one knew what Sugarloaf's "Green-Eyed Lady" was all about, but without Sugarloaf, Meat Loaf would have been unthinkable. Alive & Kicking's "Tighter, Tighter," Vanity Fare's "Hitchin' a Ride," and Edison Lighthouse's "Love Grows (Where My Rosemary Goes)" were pop masterpieces that carried on the pre-*Pepper* Beatles legacy proudly, while Bobby Bloom's "Montego Bay" added some tropical Caribbean ambience to the K-Tel experience. K-Tel's influence was also felt at Motown, where a couple of the label's white artists, Rare Earth ("Born to Wander") and R. Dean Taylor ("Indiana Wants Me"), became symbolic leaders in the ongoing battle for racial unity. Rare Earth even offered to rename themselves 'Young Black Teenagers,' but Berry Gordy felt it was "too much, too soon."

Nineteen seventy-one was a crucial transition year for pop music, and K-Tel was right there at the scene of the accident. Three Dog Night, who a year earlier took "Mama Told Me (Not To Come)" to number one and then remained a Top Forty mainstay until 1974, came up with their biggest hit ever in "Joy to the World," 1971's top single; between "Joy"'s 100-proof bullfrog Jeremiah, *Sesame Street's* beloved Kermit, and the classic Ray Milland vehicle *Frogs* (1972), America suddenly found itself targeted by an unprecedented amphibious assault. Lobo's "Me and You and a Dog Named Boo" created a worldwide scandal, not only for its hint of a clandestine *ménage à canine*, but also for the way Lobo typified the solipsistic arrogance of the one-name Warholian superstar (Madonna, Prince, Zamfir).[2] "Boo" itself was a gentle number, suggesting a rich gospel/folk/country tradition behind the average K-Tel collection that was also movingly captured by Brewer & Shipley's "One Toke Over the Line," the

[2] Tragically, Boo was killed in 1980 after a head-on collision with a Mac Truck, and to this day the singer wanders the streets a lost Lobo.

Stampeders' "Sweet City Woman," and Ocean's "Put Your Hand in the Hand." The footsteps of Hank Williams and Mahalia Jackson echoed through each: Brewer & Shipley sharing a bong with Jesus, the Stamps pining for the metropolitan thrills of Medicine Hat, Alberta, and Ocean rocking the pews and casting out sins by the truckload. Religion also figured heavily in the Five Man Electrical Band's "Signs," a vivid parable for what it must have felt like to be turned away at the inn.

The Raiders' "Indian Reservation," a devastating attack on America's genocidal past, proved that K-Tel could also embrace the more radical politics in circulation. The Raiders' disgust was especially brought home at the 1972 Academy Awards presentation, where they appeared in ceremonial Cherokee costume to pick up an award for their friend Marlon Brando. Over in the rubber room, meanwhile, Daddy Dewdrop's "Chick-a-Boom (Don't Ya Jes' Love It)" was weird, weird, weird — but not as weird as the Buoys' "Timothy," which stands alongside Hasil Adkins, Cannibal & the Headhunters, Fine Young Cannibals, and Total Coelo's "I Eat Cannibals" in the yummy subgenre of Hannibal Lecter Rock.

The K-Tel agenda for 1972 was set early when the Belgian group Chakachas hit the charts in January with "Jungle Fever," a proto-Donna Summer/Spike Lee/Plastic Bertrand orgasmatron that appalled millions. Another Nordic act, Holland's Mouth & McNeal, avoided such backlash on "How Do You Do?" by simply referring to the sex act as "na-na-na-na-na." Turning to dance music, Hot Butter's "Popcorn" became the first song ever to incorporate acid-house rhythms into a Jiffy Pop setting. Hardcore fans will also want to hear *Hot Butter Unpopped*, which contained a special acoustic remix of "Popcorn" by the band's legendary manager, Kernel Tom Parker.

K-Tel reeled in a couple of 1972's best youth anthems, too: Looking Glass's "Brandy" was a rollicking sea shanty especially popular among Newfoundland trout-fishing posses, while Gilbert O'Sullivan explored suicidal tendencies on "Alone Again (Naturally)." Erotic obsession was the focus of Mac Davis's "Baby Don't Get Hooked On Me," and certainly one look at the virile, strapping Davis made it perfectly obvious why he was turning away hungry women ten at a time. Wayne Newton, a Las Vegas legend, popped his head out of the casinos long enough to plead "Daddy Don't You Walk So Fast," then disappeared again until "Mr. Repo Man Don't You Walk So Fast" some twenty years later. Finally, nothing captured the rugged frontier spirit of the seventies better than Daniel Boone's "Beautiful Sunday," a big favorite during concerts thanks to the ritualistic 'donning of the coonskin' by the entire band.

K-Tel remained in a holding pattern for 1973, a year heavy in quality but light on quantity. Hurricane Smith reached deep into the past for "Oh Babe, What Would You Say?", updating the dearly missed Rudy Vallee sound of the 1920s; of interest to Dylanologists, Hurricane later changed his name to 'Idiot Wind' and toured as a one-man Dylan tribute band. In the field of Prussian Nihilism Rock, Deodato's "Also Sprach Zarathustra" ingeniously bridged the gap between Jack Nietzsche's "The Lonely Surfer" and Will To Power's "Say It's Gonna Rain." "Delta Dawn," one of three number-ones for Australia's Helen Reddy (flanked by "I Am Woman," 1972, and "Angie Baby," 1974), was a sinister helping of rural blues which told of a downtrodden woman knocking hard on heaven's door. Swampier still was Jim Stafford's "Spiders and Snakes," an arachnophobic howl produced by "Dog Named Boo" creator Lobo. The greatest K-Tel flag bearer in 1973, however, was Clint Holmes' "Playground in My Mind." There were a lot of other important Clints in the seventies — Clint Eastwood, Clint Howard, reserve Dallas QB Clint Longley — but none had the impact of the man who spent the summer of 1973 singing about the swings and slides that rattled around between his ears.

After the calm, the storm. Nineteen seventy-four was K-Tel's year of triumph: when Richard Nixon sits in his study nowadays pondering the cataclysmic series of events that removed him from office that fateful year, you can be sure that his memories are filtered through the distant echoes of Carl Douglas, Mocedades, and Terry Jacks, all part of an improbable soundtrack for a nation crumbling underfoot. Lunacy was so pervasive in 1974 that bands actually waged bitter cross-continental battles over the rights to prime K-Tel material. Witness the saga of "Billy, Don't Be a Hero," which was first taken to number one in Britain by the group Paper Lace, and then within a matter of weeks a version by Bo Donaldson & the Heywoods topped American charts. Paper Lace was naturally incensed, so they immediately issued a bloody hands-off warning via "The Night Chicago Died," a gangland shoot-out that similarly grabbed the number-one spot in America.

Elsewhere, the ethnic diversity of K-Tel was never richer than in 1974. The Polish community got a shot of adrenaline from Bobby Vinton's "My Melody of Love," the first major polka anthem since Lawrence Welk's "Calcutta" (1960). Blue Swede's cover of "Hooked on a Feeling" introduced 'ooga shaka, ooga shaka' into the English language (Swedish for 'wild cranberries, wild cranberries'), while Native Americans Redbone made it into the Top Ten with "Come and Get Your Love," a song they dedicated to the "tireless efforts of the Raiders in exposing the plight of the American Indian." From Spain came Mocedades, whose "Eres Tu (Touch the Wind)" sparked a meteorological craze whereby people stood in the middle of empty fields holding one finger against the breeze. K-Tel even scavenged the Far East for hit singles, where Carl Douglas (born in the far east corner of Jamaica) combined Bruce Lee films and the emerging disco sound to produce "Kung Fu Fighting," the only record ever to jump directly from platinum to black belt.

A couple of mysterious studio groups, First Class and Reunion, provided a more American sound: Britain's First Class rode the wild surf down the Thames River on "Beach Baby," while ex-Ohio Express singer Joey Levine led Reunion through "Life Is a Rock (But the Radio Rolled Me)," a rap forerunner that paid long overdue tribute to B. Bumble & the Stingers and other giants of rock. Andy Kim was another bubblegum legend who resurfaced in 1974, launching an aggressive attack on the heavy metal movement with "Rock Me Gently." Canada also gave the world Terry Jacks' "Seasons in the Sun," a Jacques Brel composition that spent three weeks at number one and later became the basis for a hit Broadway musical, *Terry Jacks Is Alive and Well and Living in Winnipeg* .

Rounding out K-Tel's highlights for the year were Ray Stevens and Sister Janet Mead, a couple of anthropological wunderkinds who exploded the myths and counter-myths of the sexual revolution. Ray celebrated one of the decade's great sex stories on "The Streak," a short-lived mania that called for removing one's clothes and running madly through public gatherings; after a sensational beginning, the psychological dangers of streaking became apparent when a quick dash across the stage by Edgar Winter shocked a defenceless concert audience into mass catatonia. Sister Janet Mead had no such inclination for erotic games: "My name ain't baby, it's Janet — Sister Mead if you're nasty," she warned on "The Lord's Prayer," a record that ranked her right alongside Father Daniel Berrigan and the Reverend Jim Jones among the seventies' preeminent spiritualists.

K-Tel started to wind down some in 1975, soon to hand over its empire to an even cheesier record label/dumpsite, but not before scooping up a handful of keepers for its vaults. The George Baker Selection's "Little Green Bag" had provided some early K-Tel thrills in 1970, and five years later an older and wiser George re-emerged with "Paloma Blanca," a polka monster that drank Bobby Vinton under the table. Labelle's "Lady Marmalade" joined Tommy Roe's "Jam Up and Jelly Tight," the MC5's "Kick Out the Jams," and Moby Grape's "Grape Jam" in the Preservative Hall of Fame, and their costumes were even fruitier. Best of all — indeed, the climactic farewell of K-Tel's wonder years — was C.W. McCall's "Convoy," a number-one trucker's anthem that paid homage to another meteoric seventies fad, the Citizen's Band Radio, in all of its boot-scootin', eighteen-wheeler glory. To paraphrase *Wayne's World*, "Convoy" was living testament to everything that was noble and visionary about Top Forty radio in the seventies — negatori!

Because the truest kind of K-Tel icon was a one-hit wonder by definition, it's almost a philosophical betrayal to nominate a multi-hit artist as best representing the label's heart and soul. If you do allow that there was such a thing as a 'K-Tel career,' however, the nod would have to go to Cher. Three Dog Night had more hits, but they were just regular guys caught up in the K-Tel maelstrom; it was Cher who, for the duration of the K-Tel epoch, stood front and centre in her ability to make people squirm and make them enjoy it. For starters there was *The Sonny & Cher Show* , where each week she was joined by a short Italian man with a moustache, and the two of them proceeded to spend an hour insulting one another's physical, intellectual, and sexual deficiencies. Then there was Cher's wardrobe, which might just as well have been designed by K-Tel's art department: Labelle without modesty, Bowie without discipline, rhyme without reason, crime without punishment, everything she wore inched us a little closer to the end of the world.

But most of all Cher was K-Tel because she made K-Tel records, three of which comprised a self-contained trilogy of deception, lust, and miscegenation that stunned the pop world like nothing since Larry Verne's "Mr. Custer." All three hit number one — "Gypsies, Tramps & Thieves" (1971), "Half Breed" (1973), and "Dark Lady" (1974) — and taken together they map the psychological landscape that made K-Tel both possible and necessary. They were part of the missing eighteen minutes on Mr. Nixon's Watergate tapes — Cher's trilogy, "Kung Fu Fighting," a couple of Bo Donaldson tunes — helping to explain why it was crucial for national security that those eighteen minutes be erased: the nation could survive a resigned presidency, but whether it could accept a president who listened to "Half Breed" and Carl Douglas, that was a Pandora's Box that dare not be opened.

The explosion of junk radio in the first half of the seventies was too all-consuming for a single chapter to contain. So far we've covered the nerve center of any given K-Tel collection, an enigmatic assortment of international nomads brought together by the marketing genius of Winnipeg's Kieves brothers. Around the edges of those K-Tel records, however, there was much else happening — things like a battalion of K-Tel understudies engaged in reinventing the generation gap all over again, urging listeners to think twice before trusting anyone over the age of thirteen.

Chapter 15

Short People Got No Reason To Live

"I'm sick of people knocking the Osmonds. I love them for their
whole teenybop thing; they're like an American version of the
early Beatles."
— Paul McCartney, 1974.

A big part of K-Tel's roots can be traced to the Monkees,
without whom there never would have been the late-sixties bubblegum
renaissance — Tommy James, the Ohio Express, 1910 Fruitgum Co.,
the Lemon Pipers — the most iridescent pop music of its day and the
backbone of multi-artist compilations put out by the Syndicate label
(an early K-Tel competitor in the cram-'em-in-sideways marketing
approach). When the Monkees petered out for good in 1969 — or
mickeyed out, or michaeled out — the torch was passed to Bobby
Sherman, a bubbleyummy mop-top from California who became
godfather to a new generation of riotous teenage pop. What
followed in his wake was a K-Tel slumber party that stayed up all
decade.

Bobby was already familiar to television viewers as Jeremy
Bolt on *Here Come the Brides*, part of the post-*Beverly Hillbillies*
hayseed cycle that included such sixties fare as *Petticoat Junction*,
Mayberry RFD, and *Green Acres*. Practically minutes after picking up

a microphone for the first time, Bobby had a Top Ten single with the fabulous "Little Woman" (1969), which sounded just like Creedence Clearwater's "Down on the Corner" for its first six seconds, except the Shermanator beat Creedence by a full two months. For the next year Bobby was an automatic on *Tiger Beat* covers, where his most private secrets became a matter of public record. In 1970, he landed a Top Ten album, *Here Comes Bobby* , and three Top Ten singles that lay to waste the tides of negativity dragging down a war-torn USA.: "La La La (If I Had You)" was good, "Easy Come, Easy Go" was better, and "Julie, Do Ya Love Me" was pure bliss. Bobby also charted a little lower that same year with "Hey Mr. Sun," the first instalment in a trilogy that included "Hey Mr. Moon" and the elaborate *Dark Side of Mr. Moon* LP.

Bobby's chart log from 1971 onward spells out 'giant slalom' in Olympic terms, a demise that could be traced to factors ranging from creative atrophy to bad karma to the immutable laws of quantum physics. The simple truth, though, was that he suddenly found himself trampled underfoot by a couple of upstart post-Manson families from the chewy underbelly of America. First up was the Partridge Family, a fictional pop group created and scripted for a weekly network television show, with a keen eye toward crossing them over onto Top Forty radio before the credits rolled on the first episode and the FCC had a chance to issue the appropriate warnings and disclaimers. They were led by David Cassidy and Shirley Jones, the only Partridges actually to appear on records and a real-life stepson/ mother combination that added a tense Freudian background to the Partridge sound. Filling out the cast were Danny Bonaduce (a wise-ass Michael J. Fox prototype and future model citizen), Susan Dey (who was beautiful and wispy and fake-played the organ with reckless abandon), a couple of mysterious little crumbcrushers for grade school ambience, and Dave Madden as manager Ruben Kincaid, who mugged and whined and sweated with frightening intensity. There was even a Partridge bus to scoot them all around, just like the one Ralph Kramden used to drive.

Soon after the show's debut, the Partridge Family had a number-one single with "I Think I Love You" (1970), one of the creepiest love ballads ever concocted. Beginning with chintzy sound-track music from a grade-Z horror film, it moved through a sordid tale of dread, insanity, and asphyxiation by pillow, paused for a jazzy Bach-like instrumental rave-up, and finished with David hammering home the song's title in a frenzied call-and-response between himself and his addled conscience. The Partridges never matched "I Think I Love You" for sheer audacity, but the rest of their debut album was absolutely first-rate, and in 1971 they followed with a couple more Top Ten hits, "Doesn't Somebody Want To Be Wanted" and "I'll Meet You Half-way." Their TV show lasted through four seasons of Danny's madcap scheming and Reuben's perpetual slow-burn, until they were finally pink-slipped in 1973, with the entire family piling into their bus and driving it over a cliff for the final episode.

As dazzling as the Partridges and Bobby Sherman were, neither of them seriously challenged the Jackson 5's chart supremacy during 1970 and 1971. But in early 1971, the Jacksons finally met their match in the Osmonds, a posse of fast-steppin' Mormons from the cornfields of Utah. Battle lines were immediately drawn, and not since the Beatles and the Stones slugged it out in the mid-sixties would the pop community become so sharply divided in its allegiances and prejudices.

The Osmonds story begins with record producer and pop visionary Mike Curb, who according to legend was so impressed with the Jackson 5 that he set himself the task of cloning them according to his own eccentric specifications: "If only I could find five Mormon brothers from Utah with the Jackson 5 sound and the Jackson 5 feel, I could one day get myself elected to the California State Assembly." As luck would have it, Curb didn't have to look any further than television's The Andy Williams Show, where the five Osmond brothers had been performing semi-regularly since the early-sixties. (The four oldest Osmonds, Wayne, Merle, Bucky, and Sleepy, made their debut in 1962, with younger brother Donny joining them on Dec. 10, 1963, less than three weeks after JFK's assassination; this is known as the "fifth Osmond theory" in some quarters.) Without a moment's hesitation, Curb scooped up his ready-made protégés and went to work.

The first Osmonds single under Curb's direction was the spectacularly overripe "One Bad Apple" (1971), which indeed had the Jackson 5 sound and the Jackson 5 feel to spare. Holding down the number-one slot for five straight weeks, "One Bad Apple" was the gateway to an Osmond empire that stunned the world for the next half-decade. Anchoring this multi-pronged attack was Donny, who besides being the focal point of Osmonds records proper, also had major chart success on his own, resurrecting twilight-time classics from Steve Lawrence ("Go Away Little Girl," 1971), Freddie Scott ("Hey Girl," 1971), and Johnny Mathis ("Twelfth of Never," 1973).

Meanwhile, Donny and his brothers were turning into seething hard-rock madmen: 1971's "Yo-Yo" was their masterpiece, while "Down By the Lazy River" and "Crazy Horses" (both 1972) suggested a secret Osmond-Neil Young connection heretofore unexplored. That same year, the pint-sized Little Jimmy Osmond got into the act, hitting number one in the U.K. with his completely preposterous "Long Haired Lover From Liverpool." Jimmy had freckles, was less than eleven inches tall, and still owes his family and the rest of the world an apology.

When the Osmond juggernaut started to slow down some in 1973, sister Marie Osmond climbed aboard to spark a final phase of distaff glory with "Paper Roses," a song originally made famous by closet orange juice queen Anita Bryant. In 1976, the Osmond saga culminated where it once began, on a TV variety hour, when *The Donny & Marie Show* introduced a whole new way of thinking into the American political debate, deciding a presidential election that very same year: running on a platform of 'A Little Bit Country,' Jimmy Carter took on Gerald Ford, the 'A Little Bit Rock 'n' Roll' incumbent, and booted him right out of office.

Bobby, David, and Donny were the teen idols of the seventies nearest and dearest to our own hearts, but there were others whose impact cannot be overlooked. Leading the way were the Bay City Rollers, five tartan-toothed ding-a-lings from Scotland who were the missing Kilt Rock link between Harry Lauder and W. Axl Rose. Rollermania was a seventies phenomenon as real and indelible as the hula-hoop craze of 1958 or the Tylenol scare of 1982 (with certain affinities to both); it swept through North America in the fall of 1975, having already knocked Britain senseless, and stayed strong till the winter of 1976, an unprecedented reign. The Rollers hit number one in the U.S. with "Saturday Night" (1975), an oi-like invocation to weekend warriors that wore its spell-checker on its sleeve. Of their half-dozen hits that followed, the best were "Rock and Roll Love Letter" (1976), a power-pop howitzer, and "Yesterday's Hero" (1976), the band's admission of panic over their ultimate place in history — not to worry, lads, we remember!

Meanwhile, relegated to the back of the school bus was a fascinating collection of truants and problem children. Especially mischievous was the DeFranco Family, a Canadian export whose "Heartbeat — It's a Lovebeat" (1973) earned them a permanent niche alongside the Dimaggios, the Espositos, and the Corleones in the annals of Italian folklore. The Sylvers, a pet project of ex-Jackson 5 producer Freddie Perren, was another family outfit eager to parade its dirty laundry in public. On their bicentennial trilogy of "Boogie Fever," "Cotton Candy," and "Hot Line," the Sylvers made it clear that sex and cocaine and celebrity guest-lists were OK, but disco wasn't really disco without a full fifteen-minute recess.

The Partridge legacy was rekindled in the late seventies by David's younger brother Shaun, who began on TV as one-half of detective team *The Hardy Boys*. After making the Top Ten three times in 1977 with "Da Doo Ron Ron," "That Is Rock and Roll," and "Hey Deanie," Shaun promptly reverted to character and arrested himself as a public nuisance. Leif Garrett, who played Sheriff Buford Pusser's interior decorator in all three *Walking Tall* films, followed Shaun's lead by covering "Surfin' USA" and "Runaround Sue" (both 1977), after which he frugged himself into the Top Ten with "I Was Made for Dancin'" from his popular *Liege and Leif* LP (1978). And don't forget 'Tyrannosaurus' Rex Smith, who roamed the earth mightily around the time of "You Take My Breath Away" (1979) before being declared officially extinct within a couple of years.

With all this unbridled youthful energy unleashed during the seventies, it was more important than ever that pop music come forward with an equal share of positive role models and sagacious elder statesmen. Bobby Sherman, Leif Garrett, Little Jimmy Osmond — they and the rest didn't just emerge from a vacuum, they needed guidance and inspiration from above, a sense of self and purpose that even the likes of Mike Curb and Shirley Jones couldn't provide. Fortunately the K-Tel revolution was fully manned at both ends of the age spectrum, giving rise to an exciting new movement that ran parallel to the teen-pop takeover: the birth of Adult Contemporary, or Why We Have Radio Stations Today That Think Celine Dion and Peabo Bryson Make a Cute Couple.

Chapter 16

Mommy's All Right, Daddy's All Right, They Just Seem a Little Weird

"I know I could play rock 'n' roll drums as well as anybody, but I don't get off as much playing just that anymore. I'm looking for sensitivity, which rock 'n' roll lacks. Some people find that hard to understand."
— Danny Seraphine of Chicago, 1973.

JUNK radio in the 1970s had something for everyone. The 'big tent' theory prevailed, a phrase that took on a distinct double meaning during the K-Tel years. It was not only the kind of tent that housed clowns and elephants and fire-eaters (fill in the guilty parties yourself), but also the kind that politicians yammer about, that embraces white people and black people, working people and rich people, fun people and people who watch a lot of German cinema, young people and old people, and everyone in between. Therefore, in order to complement the Partridge Family and the rest of the teen pop storm-troopers, Top Forty radio had to open its tent to the over-thirties and over-forties in the audience and bring all the moms, dads, and future 'Sweatin' to the Oldies' members into its fold. This widening of the demographic laid the foundation for what is now known in radio circles as 'Adult Contemporary,' but which went under the name of 'Easy Listening' in the seventies. (The name change became necessary because, as anyone who was around in the seventies knows, there was nothing very 'easy' about John Denver's "Thank God I'm a Country Boy," Barry Manilow's "Copacabana," and other equally supercharged blitz-kriegs). It is here that we make a solemn pledge: of all the chapters in this book, this is the one that's not too hard, not too soft.

The Easy Listening format got rolling in the seventies with Karen and Richard Carpenter, a brother and sister team from California who, with the release of "(They Long To Be) Close to You" (1970), helped invent the decade that lay ahead just as surely as "Paranoid," "Mama Told Me (Not To Come)," "Indiana Wants Me," and all the other weird-sounding flotsam and jetsam circulating at the time. The Carpenters mortified early-seventies rock fans, making them wonder if they were being punished for some terrible, unnameable sin. But as they wondered, the exquisite beauty of "Close to You" snuck up and sprinkled moondust in their hair, and they began to ponder other, much deeper questions: Why did birds suddenly appear? Why did stars fall down from the sky? Why weren't their parents asking them to turn down the radio anymore? Sometimes the Carpenters were sad and wistful and brilliant ("We've Only Just Begun," 1970; "Rainy Days and Mondays" and "Superstar," 1971), sometimes they reared back and drove seven-inch nails into your forehead ("Sing" and "Top of the World," 1973). But they remained true to themselves until the end — they never did glam, they never did disco, they never did a live album. They did travel a lonely, melancholy road that took them from a Beatles cover ("Ticket to Ride," 1970) to a Klaatu cover ("Calling Occupants," 1977). We will never hear their like again.

Another important carpenter was Jesus, who in zero A.D. held a famous shindig where he gave all the guests bread and wine. Although there wasn't a band named Wine in the Easy Listening genre (April Wine doesn't count, they 'rocked too hard'), there was one named Bread that was almost as influential as the Carpenters in setting the tone for what followed. Bread made it into the Top Ten five times in the space of three years, highlighted by "Make It With You" (1970) and "Everything I Own" (1972), even though every good divorce lawyer knows that you give someone everything you own to get rid of them, not get them back.

Three early Easy Listening powerhouses were John Denver,

Tony Orlando & Dawn, and Roberta Flack. Mountain-boy Denver rang up four number-one singles by tapping into the eco-consciousness of Deep Purple and Bo Donaldson fans hungry for shared environmental responsibility among citizens. John sang guilelessly about rural infra-structure ("Take Me Home, Country Roads," 1971), rural fresh air ("Rocky Mountain High", 1973; "Sunshine on My Shoulders," 1974), and rural domesticity ("Annie's Song," 1974), and on "Thank God I'm a Country Boy" (1975) he rustled up a three-course rural breakfast at breakneck speed. Tony Orlando & Dawn had more of an urban, blue collar appeal, a gritty New York immediacy best captured on "Candida" and "Knock Three Times" (both 1970). Dawn peaked with their 1973 vaudeville trilogy — "Tie a Yellow Ribbon Round the Ole Oak Tree," "Say, Has Anybody Seen My Sweet Gypsy Rose," and "Who's in the Strawberry Patch With Sally"— but fell victim to a massive boycott from easy listeners after the hardcore disco rhythms of "Steppin' Out (Gonna Boogie Tonight)" (1974). The genre's most prominent black voice belonged to Roberta Flack, whose "The First Time Ever I Saw Your Face" (1972) remains the prettiest song ever culled from a Clint Eastwood film (*Play Misty For Me*), prettier even than "Love Theme from *Dirty Harry* ." Roberta also caused a stir with "Killing Me Softly With His Song" (1973), which, like "You're So Vain," had everyone trying to guess who she was singing about — Don McLean, it turned out, though early speculation centered around either Hamilton, Joe Frank, or Reynolds.

Easy Listening's most consistent presence through the years has been Chicago, *Billboard* 's third biggest hitmakers of the seventies behind Elton John and Paul McCartney. They began the decade as one of the elephantine jazz-rock congregations then coming into vogue (Blood, Sweat & Tears, Lighthouse, Ides of March), but starting with "Just You 'n' Me" (1973) they purged themselves of their musical demons and settled into a quieter, more reflective, flute-driven phase that climaxed with "If You Leave Me Now" (1976). They're most famous, perhaps, for titling all their albums with Roman numerals: *Chicago X* (1973), a prescient tribute to Malcolm X; *Chicago XXX* (1976), a salacious collaboration with Xaviera Hollander; and *Chicago XOX* (1979), a Dixieland opera about tic-tac-toe, were especially noteworthy.

Chicago's fiercest competitor in the big-band division of Easy Listening was America, a guitar-mad trio that brought a quality of raging gothic doom to the genre not heard again until Yes's "Owner of a Lonely Heart" in 1983. America first gained notice as uncanny Neil Young soundalikes on 1972's "A Horse With No Name," but "Ventura Highway" (1972), "Tin Man" (1974), and 1975's "Sister Golden Hair" (inspired by Goldie Hawn's performance in *Shampoo*) were Easy Listening through and through. America had an album-title gimmick of its own, beginning each and every one with the letter H: *Homecoming* (1972), *Holiday* (1974), *Horticulture* (1976), and *Horn of Plenty* (1977) were but a few.

Barbara Streisand, Diana Ross, and Neil Diamond comprised the aristocracy of 1970s Easy Listening, three veterans who'd outgrown their Broadway/girl-group/bubblepunk roots and now served as viable role models for the Merle Osmonds and Nino DeFrancos of the youth-cult industry. Barbara was actually more concerned with making films in the seventies, but her multi-media blitz came together swimmingly when the title song from *The Way We Were* went to number one in 1974. Three more number-one singles followed: "Evergreen" in 1976, about a tiny Peruvian shrub she adopted; "You Don't Bring Me Flowers" in 1978, an experimental duet with Neil Diamond that was sung from a corpse's point of view; and "No More Tears (Enough Is Enough)" in 1979, a disco duet with Donna Summer.

Diana Ross initially looked backward to Motown's heyday for material (a cover of "Ain't No Mountain High Enough" was her first solo number-one in 1970), and later she sunk her claws firmly into disco, but for the greater middle part of the decade she was a fragile, twittering songbird, a Tammy Faye Bakker forerunner with mile-high teeth and eyelashes to spare. Diana's two biggest ballads were "Touch Me in the Morning" (1973), which joined Cat Stevens' "Morning Has Broken" and Maureen McGovern's "The Morning After" in the crucial 'Morning Sickness Trilogy' of 1972-73, and "Theme from Mahogany (Do You Know Where You're Going To)" (1975).

Neil Diamond began the 1970s mired in youth revolt, as "Cracklin' Rosie" (1970) typified the sudden wave of drinking-binge rants then infiltrating Top Forty ("Joy to the World," "Spill the Wine," the Guess Who's "New Mother Nature"). But "Song Sung Blue" (1972) revealed a more contemplative Neil, a brooding sonnet-master given full reign on his soundtrack for the smash existentialist comedy *Jonathan Livingston Sea Creature* (1973). Neil settled into Easy Listening once and for all after that, spinning rich tales of knightly chivalry and ritualistic courtship, and on "Longfellow Serenade" (1974) he explored cute nicknames for one's sexual apparatus.

Of the Adult Contemporary pioneers who came of age in the seventies, the most popular by the middle of the decade were Olivia Newton-John, Barry Manilow, and Captain & Tennille. Australia's Olivia Newton-John, a second cousin to Elton and the step-niece of Wayne Newton, captured the hearts of millions with the wistful romanticism of "I Honestly Love You" (1974), "Have You Never Been Mellow" (1975), and "Please Mr. Please" (1975). In contrast to her fellow countrywoman Helen Reddy, whose "I Am Woman" was a manifesto of hard-headed militancy, Olivia came across as a soft, vulnerable, cuddly marsupial, a teensy-tiny whisper in the long K-Tel night. ONJ continued to coo and suck her thumb until 1978, when she donned black leather for the film *Grease* and erotically twined herself around John Travolta on "You're the One That I Want." It was a transformation that shocked the entire Easy Listening community.

Barry Manilow's career began as musical director for Bette Midler during her gay bathhouse days, so rest assured it took more than a little playful bondage to shock him. Starting with 1974's "Mandy," Barry became a permanent fixture in the American cultural landscape, a combination Jimmy Durante/Carmen Miranda dynamo who walked a fine line between Ziggy Stardust glitter-theatre and Stephen Sondheim showtune-follies. Barry's biggest ballads were "I Write the Songs" (1975) and "Looks Like We Made It" (1977), but he's most loved for "Copacabana (at the Copa)" from 1978, a full helping of his song-and-dance magic that resurrected the long-lost spirit of Ricky Ricardo.

Captain & Tennille embodied the *Love Boat* aesthetic of the mid-seventies: Daryl Dragon took on Captain Stubing's role, his lovely wife Toni Tennille was an even perkier Julie, and though they didn't have Gopher on hand for madcap comic relief, they did satisfy their rodent quotient by covering America's "Muskrat Love" in 1976. The duo caused an immediate sensation with their debut single "Love Will

106

Keep Us Together," which celebrated an emotion so powerful and universal it spawned hit versions in Spanish ("Por Amor Viveremos"), Japanese ("Ninjen No Joken"), and Nadsat ("Devotchkas Slooshying"). Each of their next four singles also went into the Top Ten, and when wholesomeness was no longer enough, they followed Olivia into soft-core pornography by employing the most lurid prepositions imaginable on "You Never Done It Like That" (1978) and "Do That to Me One More Time" (1979) — 'it,' 'that,' who did they think they were fooling?

Easy Listening chart successes rampantly multiplied as the decade progressed. Paul Anka ("You're Having My Baby," 1974), Neil Sedaka ("Laughter in the Rain," 1974), Minnie Riperton ("Lovin' You," 1975), Melissa Manchester ("Midnight Blue," 1975), Seals & Crofts ("Get Closer," 1976), England Dan & John Ford Coley ("I'd Really Love To See You Tonight," 1976), and countless others ensured that pop music would never be completely overtaken by sin and licentiousness, that there would always be the gentle hand of maturity and temperance to steady its course. It was Brazilian export Morris Albert who captured the elusive appeal of Easy Listening better than anyone on 1975's anthemic "Feelings": "Feelings/Nothing more than feelings/Trying to forget my/Feelings of love." When asked by *Rolling Stone* how he came to write such a stark confession, Morris explained that "I was at a low ebb both physically and emotionally, my career going nowhere and Pelé slumping badly, and it suddenly overwhelmed me how life begins and ends at the most fundamental level of all, our feelings, and how those feelings are either nurtured or destroyed by love. Something like that anyway — I wrote it three months ago."

Easy Listening moves in cycles. Many of its founders, the Morris Alberts and the Toni Tennilles of yesteryear, have faded out of the picture by now, but just as many of the 1970s' most outlandish characters — Elton, Cher, Rod Stewart — are well established on today's Easy Listening/Adult Contemporary playlists. Some artists, the Rolling Stones and Ozzy Osbourne for instance, are even able to move comfortably back and forth between Adult Contemporary and Album-Oriented Hard Rock stations. The coming together of generations in the 1990s is very encouraging.

Chapter 17

ABBA, ABBA, WE ACCEPT YOU, WE ACCEPT YOU, ONE OF US

"I remember hearing 'SOS' on the radio in the States and realizing
that it was ABBA. But it was too late, because I was already
transported by it."
— Pete Townshend, 1982.

THERE was one story in the 1970s that resonated with such
clarity it's a wonder that *Time* and *Newseek* didn't fall all over each
other trying to get there first: the Swedish Invasion that swept across
North America in the mid-to-late seventies. Within a few years, Bjorn
Borg emerged as the world's number-one tennis player, Borje Salming
reintroduced chivalrous conduct to the increasingly Neanderthal sport
of hockey, film director Ingmar Bergman released his comedy-adven-
ture epic *The Serpent's Egg*, and Lillian Muller won *Playboy* 's 1975
Playmate of the Year award. We could continue throwing names at
you, but there's really no point — as invasions go, that's a lot of frontline resonance right there.

The acknowledged focal point of this powerhouse Nordic
takeover was ABBA, the consummate bubble-pop-tee-vee-toon band
of the decade, the sexiest Swedish export since *I Am Curious (Yellow)*,
and one of only four groups in history whose name was a palindrome

(M, Q, and X were the others).[1] Between 1974 and 1980, ABBA racked up thirteen Top Forty singles in America, a figure that paled next to their totals in Europe and in more remote corners of the universe — only Elvis, the Beatles, and Cliff Richard had more number-ones in Great Britain, and not one of them had to go head-to-head with C.W. McCall and Bimbo Jet. Indeed, ABBA was a perfect pop bridge between the K-Tel clowns of the early seventies and the disco ducks who took over three-quarters of the way through, a historical service that must never be forgotten — after all, a culture that transfers allegiance from Paper Lace and Clint Holmes to Meco and the Village People is a potentially volatile culture, with who knows what kind of incipient ugliness waiting to explode.

To North Americans observing the Swedish music scene of the late sixties (a 1969 census pegged the number at somewhere around three), ABBA's eventual world domination was not that surprising. By the time Benny Anderson, Bjorn Ulvaeus, Agnetha Faltskog, and Anni-Frid Lyngstad hooked up together in 1969, all of them had achieved some measure of success in their native land, either solo or with other groups. Benny Anderson even qualified as a pop celebrity of sorts, scoring fifteen chart hits with a group called the Hep Stars. Somewhat inexplicably, the name Hep Stars has not been resurrected in the intervening years.

Someone who played a major role in launching this new foursome was manager Stig Anderson, often called "the fifth ABBA." Besides possessing a classic rock and roll name in his own right — with strong intimations of 'Sting', 'Stiv', 'Styx', and 'Lynn Anderson' — it was Stig who came up with the name ABBA in 1974. Much like the twentieth-century art movement Dada, 'ABBA' has multiple meanings and has been subjected to almost as many interpretations: in Sweden the name is linguistically similar to a popular brand of pickled herring; Stig maintains it was generated by rearranging the members' first initials; musicologists claim that A-B-B-A is a precise denotation of the band's songwriting structure; retailers were convinced it was a clever

---

[1] Actually, ABBA boasted a uniquely inside-out double-reverse palindrome, but that probably isn't worth pursuing in any great detail.

ploy to get ABBA records racked at the front of record bins; number-one fan Pete Townshend probably thought it was a reference to "Baba O'Riley"; we haven't got a clue, we only know it's easy to spell.

Also in 1974, Benny's and Bjorn's "Waterloo" was chosen to be Sweden's entry in the annual Eurovision song contest, the song-writer's equivalent of a beauty pageant, minus the swimsuit and congeniality competitions. When the song took first prize against long odds, rabid Swedes took to the streets in celebration, and from that day forward ABBA never looked back. "Waterloo" went on to hit number six in America, with rolling piano bits and a sprightly saxophone recalling the Crystals' "Da Doo Ron Ron"; that ABBA scooped both Bruce Springsteen *and* Shaun Cassidy in plundering the Crystals only confirms their place among the industry's giants.

One hot ABBA rumor right from the get-go was that none of its members spoke English, and therefore they had to learn their lyrics phonetically. If this was true, and it's never been confirmed one way or the other, we personally don't see it as a big deal. For starters, phonetic learning of lyrics would make ABBA the direct forbears of Milli Vanilli's Rob Pilatus and Fab Morvan, who had the even tougher task of not-learning their lyrics phonetically, and managed to not-author one of 1989's best albums anyway. It all evens out in the end.

ABBA stayed strong in 1975 with "SOS," a record that would have been better situated during the heyday of corporate sponsorship a decade later: it was a natural for those people who make steel-wool pads, especially as the typical ABBA hit sounded like a commercial jingle anyway. "I Do, I Do, I Do, I Do, I Do" (1976 — we don't, by the way) had a vaudevillian feel to it, falling somewhere between Sly Stone's "Hot Fun in the Summertime" and Hurricane Smith's "Oh Babe, What Would You Say?" Somewhere along the way there were a couple of internal marriages and divorces, the exact sequence not important, the upshot being that ABBA joined Fleetwood Mac in the 'anybody-wanna-swap-wives-tonight?' parade. The imaginations of lonely adolescents such as ourselves worked overtime.

Certain trademarks anchored ABBA's sound throughout the seventies — huge choruses, dancehall pianos, tambourines, glockenspiels, kazoos, bird calls — but their stylistic versatility was astonishing. Like so many others of their era, they made their biggest splash with a disco record, 1977's "Dancing Queen," which was actually more *about* disco than part of it (which is not to say that people didn't dance to it anyway, unless they were just dancing *about* it). To this day the debate rages over who "Dancing Queen" was addressed to: some say disco queen Donna Summer, others say disco queen Sylvester, while others say rock Sylvesters Queen, who were edging closer to disco themselves at the time. Whatever the case, there's no denying that ABBA communicated best to the world through tinny speakers blasting out Top Forty, and to that end "Dancing Queen" was their only single to reach number one in America.

ABBA continued to chart hits for the rest of the decade with "Knowing Me, Knowing You" (1977), "Take a Chance on Me" (1978), and "Does Your Mother Know" (1979), remaining surprisingly immune to an army of punks who were out to destroy the band and everything they stood for ("I hate ABBA!" proclaimed a T-shirt worn by Johnny Rotten; "No More ABBA in 1977!" ranted Joe Strummer). But fittingly, eerily even, it all ended as a new decade began. ABBA's last Top Ten hit, "The Winner Takes It All" (1980), was just another pop tune with a tough-luck lyric on the surface, but on closer inspection it can be read as a despondent farewell to their audience:

> I don't wanna talk about things we've gone through
> Though it's hurting me, now it's history
> I played all my cards, and that's what you've done too
> Nothing more to say, no more ace to play

There *is* nothing more to say. Goodbjye, bjeautiful friends, goodbjye.

Chapter 18

Toto Recall

"Poco had Hollywood set on fire when they were first together.
I've told you before about how I used to hang around them and
watch them rehearse with my mouth hanging open."
— Glenn Frey, 1973.

Pop music in the mid-seventies was like the comings and goings
in *One Flew Over the Cuckoo's Nest*, winner of the Oscar for Best Film
of 1975: aberrant behavior as a daily routine, a surplus of arm-
flapping, eye-rolling, and wheeling around in circles, an imperious
Indian cooly surveying the surrounding bedlam (either Redbone,
Cher, or the Raiders' Mark Lindsay), and a terrifying nurse keeping
watch from behind the admitting desk (Don Kirshner). Weird but
lively, in other words, and once inside it felt as if you'd never get out.
Much weirdness lay ahead in the late seventies, too, but to ease
ourselves safely there, it's best to gear down a little first, run down the
road and loosen our load, hasten down the wind till the wind don't
blow no more. 'Mellowing out' it's called in seventies-speak, meaning
an even more spiritually advanced state of mellowness than that
envisioned by Donovan, Olivia Newton-John, or Barry Mellowmow.
People mellowed far and wide in the 1970s, but nowhere did they
mellow harder or faster than in California. Pass out the thorazine,

Nurse Ratched, we're headin' west.

Front and center for this Great California Mold Rush was the Eagles, an L.A. band whose wingspan stretched majestically from the early-seventies heyday of Poco, Malo, and Charo to the late-seventies influx into California of deranged punk rock miscreants like the Plimsouls and the Cretones. The Eagles first hit in 1972 with "Take It Easy," a joyous memoir of how the guys once won a closely contested footrace with seven women, introduced by some of the most bracing chords found on any pop single of the decade .[1] By the time of "Best of My Love" (1974), the first of five number-one singles for the band, they began to assume an identity as evocative and powerful as their ornithological brethren the Wings and the Partridge Family: rough and tumble desperados roaming the boutiques and freeways of Hollywood Hills, anti-image/anti-celebrity/anti-media publicity hounds, and inventors of a brooding California mythos that still reverberates today with memory, desire, and the tribal rhythms of wickedly witchy women and their wascly wabbits. "One of These Nights," "Lyin' Eyes," and "Take It to the Limit" (all 1975) stood out like pillars of roguish yet sensitive manliness on Top Forty playlists of the day, giving both shape and substance to the phrase "play that funky music, white boy." It all came together brilliantly on 1977's *Hotel California*, the Eagles' ultimate metaphor for a subculture that was imploding in the face of sex, cocaine, encounter groups, anomie, ennui, entropy, A-B-C, 1-2-3, baby you and me. The album's key song, "Life in the Fast Lane," laid it on the line for all to hear: "I'm a hard-headed man, I'm a cruel dude, I've surely lost my mind/Life in the fast lane/Bleah."

The Eagles got their start in 1971 as backup band for Linda Ronstadt, a future West Coast goddess on the order of Suzanne Somers, Barbi Benton, and Patty Hearst. Linda drifted along uneventfully until 1974, but after *Heart Like a Wheel* and "You're No Good" both made it to number one, her album covers immediately joined those of Olivia and Carly as the favorite bedtime reading of creative adolescent males everywhere. Both songs were cover versions, a shortcut to glory that Ronstadt and her producer Peter Asher pursued with uncommon zeal and no discernible modesty. They appropriated hit singles from Martha and the Vandellas ("Heatwave," 1975), Buddy

[1] An A, a D, and a truncated F# if memory serves.

Holly ("That'll Be the Day," 1976), Roy Orbison ("Blue Bayou," 1977), the Rolling Stones ("Tumbling Dice," 1978), Chuck Berry ("Back in the U.S.A.," 1978), and Smokey Robinson ("Ooh Baby Baby," 1978) — only the works of the Beatles, William Faulkner, and Mahatma Gandhi were left untouched. It was a winning strategy all around, as these were songs that clearly needed to be covered; Linda brought new depths of awareness to them, a probing wisdom that went far beyond the originals, most likely explained by her ongoing romance with California Governor Jerry Brown, one of the 1970s' most poetic, compassionate, and visionary crackpots.

The third vertice in California's Self-Help Triangle of the 1970s was Fleetwood Mac. (The second version of Fleetwood Mac, that is, the one that came after the late-sixties British blues band that saw two of its members defect to religious sects, the kind of thing that's bound to happen to Amy Grant and Stryper one day.) By 1975 the band had relocated to L.A., adding Lindsey Buckingham and Stevie Nicks to the lineup and bringing the refurbished Fleetwood Mac very close to the Fleetwoods of the 1950s ("Come Softly to Me," "Mr. Blue") in both sound and style. The only difference was that the Fleetwoods were well-behaved teenagers who kept their mitts off each other, something the orgy-crazed Fleetwood Macs found impossible.

Their commercial breakthrough came with 1975's *Fleetwood Mac*, which produced the hit singles "Over My Head," "Rhiannon," and "Say You Love Me," dreamy, sexy approximations of what happens to the human spirit when it's trapped inside flowing caftans and feathered hats in 105-degree temperatures. *Rumors* (1977), their next album, sent them right off the chart: twenty million copies sold, thirty-one weeks at number one, four Top Ten singles, and an all-consuming presence in everyday American life as powerful as disco, *Star Wars*, and Mayor McCheese. After two years off and a seven-way wife swap, the band pumped their untold riches into the eccentric but ill-fated *Tusk* (1979), remembered today because its title track was recorded inside a U.S.C. Trojan huddle before a crucial third-and-long play.

The Doobie Brothers and Jefferson Starship, a couple of bands that operated in the shadow of the big three, also learned how to mellow productively after a period of gestation, transmogrification, and mutation similar to Fleetwood Mac's. The Doobies, who should not be confused with either the dB's (early-eighties power pop) or Dumbo (late-forties flying elephant), began their glorious trek into narcolepsy as an HRS fountainhead. "Long Train Runnin'" and "China Grove" (both 1973) were Kodiak-and-flannel classics, while "Black Water" (1975) was the decade's most startling swamp music to bubble up from beside a suburban sprinkler puddle. After the addition of Michael McDoobie in 1975, however, the band took the Tower of Power pledge and began to favor saxophones and keyboards over guitars. "Takin' It to the Streets" (1976) premiered an exciting new sophistication in the previously untameable Brothers, a makeover that was completed in 1979 with "What a Fool Believes" and "Minute by Minute." Doobie or not Doobie? It was the question then, it's the question now.

Jefferson Starship was the name adopted in 1974 by former mushroom-chomping militants Jefferson Airplane, who after a great start in 1970 with "Mexico" were pretty much puttering around on empty by the middle of the decade. But when original member Marty Balin rejoined the group for 1975's *Red Octopus*, a surprise huge seller, they became aligned with a different kind of revolution, the Adult Contemporary revolution, and caught second wind. On "Miracles" (1975), "With Your Love" (1976), and "Count on Me" (1978), the band explored increasingly magnificent vistas of empty interstellar space, until finally they were secure enough in their new demographic to become simply Starship. Klingons were a recurring problem throughout this sensitive transition period.

Interconnected with the West Coast feeding frenzy, but situated morosely outside it, were a couple of mainstays from the early-seventies singer-songwriter contingent, Jackson Browne and Neil Young. Browne, a former teenage prodigy whose compositions uncovered emotional affinities between the Eagles ("Take It Easy"), the Jackson 5 ("Doctor My Eyes"), and Nico ("These Days"), was a special favorite of friendless mopers for *Late for the Sky* (1974) and *The Pretender* (1976). In Martin Scorsese's *Taxi Driver* (1976), for instance, Robert De Niro's Travis Bickle character found himself so overwhelmed by the sorrowful plaint of Jackson's voice that he kicked over a TV set, bought himself a stockpile of weaponry, and set out on a mission to put Browne out of his misery once and for all. Jackson loosened up considerably for *Running on Empty* (1977), even earning a couple of spry hit singles with the title track and a cover of the Zodiacs' "Stay," after which he hooked up with actress Daryl Hannah and was sad no more.

Neil Young's mid-seventies output was a surefire way to take the fun out of almost anything, including sitting around feeling sorry for yourself (which can sometimes be extremely fun). *Time Fades Away* (1973), *On the Beach* (1974), and *Tonight's the Night* (1975) were such downers that they were legally classified as depressants and sold through pharmacies on a prescription basis only. Neil's later releases *Zuma* (1975), *American Stars 'n Bars* (1977), and *Comes a Time* (1978) got progressively cheerier, and on *Rust Never Sleeps* (1979) he shocked many by pogoing around madly and expressing eternal fealty to the punk rock movement: "The King is gone and we're really hurtin'/This is the story of Plastic Bertrand."

The West Coast also had its share of droller types: Randy Newman, Tonio K, Tommy Lasorda, and, for our purposes, Steely Dan and Warren Zevon. Steely Dan, essentially a two-man band led by Donald Fagen and Walter Becker, took the concept of 'studio craftsmanship' to prohibitive levels of monomania. Whereas even Tangerine Dream liked to load up the old tour bus once in a while and take their music to the people, Fagen and Becker and their revolving door of hired help rarely set foot outside the studio for fear of encountering 'random human interaction' and other such natural disasters. Dan's early albums and singles were good enough to justify this self-imposed isolation, especially "Reeling in the Years" (1973), *Pretzel Logic* (1974), and *Katy Lied* (1975). By the time of *Aja* (1977), however, Fagen and Becker had just about lost all contact with the flow of everyday life.

Warren Zevon's *Excitable Boy* caused a great deal of commotion in 1978, partly because of its big-name supporting cast (Linda Ronstadt, Jackson Browne, Mick Fleetwood, 'Jim Dandy' Souther), but mostly for the way it brought a slightly deranged sensibility to L.A. pop. Well, at least taken in context it did — next to Jackson Browne and Glenn Frey, Alastair Cooke could have titled an album *Excitable Boy* and gotten away with it. The LP's undisputed masterpiece was "Werewolves of London," which bayed and howled and joined Five

Man Electrical Band's "Werewolf" (1974), the Guess Who's "Clap for the Wolfman" (1974), and the New York Dolls' "Personality Crisis" in the seventies' lycanthropy division.

Like so many seventies genres, West Coast pop got really crazy down in the trenches. There was a mystery, a daring, and an unquenchable search for universal truths in the music of Dan Fogelberg, Stonebolt, Firefall, Karla Bonoff, and Ambrosia that rang out defiantly against the late-seventies landscape. Rickie Lee Jones made a bid for the pages of *Downbeat* with "Chuck E.'s in Love" (1978), even going so far as to smoke lots of cigarettes, wear a beret at a jaunty angle, and pretend to like Tom Waits. Rarely has one woman penetrated the bohemian experience so deeply. Nicolette Larson won a Grammy in 1978 for "Lotta Love," an abridged version of the Led Zeppelin classic, while the slashing power chords and multi-layered harmonies of Toto's "Hold the Line" (1978) earned them a niche in history alongside Kansas, America ("Tin Man"), and John Mellencamp ("Rain on the Scarecrow") in the ever-expanding field of Wizard-of-Oz Rock. And what is there left to say about Pablo Cruise's "Whatcha Gonna Do?" (1977) and "Love Will Find a Way" (1978) that hasn't already been said a million times before? How about that Pablo Cruise is not related to Tom Cruise, or at least there's no documentation to support such a claim? That hardly ever gets said.

The special genius of those long-ago days on the Coast did not dry up when the seventies ended, though never again was there such a concentration of kindred spirits in one place and one time, a brotherly and sisterly network of drugstore ploughboys, reclusive eccentrics, and practising somnambulists, all of them united behind the inimitable session work of Jeff 'Skunk' Baxter, Danny Kortchmar, and Waddy Wachtel. Journey and Toto carried the torch into the 1980s, it was passed to Huey Lewis and Bruce Hornsby later in the decade, and today the tradition is carried on proudly by M.C. Hammer. Some dance to remember, some dance to forget.

Chapter 19

SOME PEOPLE CALL ME MAURICE

"We do carry on before going on. We stand in a circle and hold
hands and we basically kind of communicate to each other. We
all say a prayer, each in our own way, and then we join the forces
of harmony and go out and do what we do."
— Maurice White of Earth, Wind & Fire, 1978.

As tempting as it is to suggest that the slumbering, studio-
spellbound state of mid-seventies pop was the exclusive domain of
wealthy white rock stars from L.A., the truth is there was a kind of
hush all over the world by 1975. Funk and reggae, two black styles
that flourished at the time, picked up the pieces of soul music after it
followed John Shaft's various nemeses to the grave and proved that
Jefferson Starship and Firefall were hardly isolated phenomena. Funk
artists spent months, sometimes years, pursuing heady concepts and
mixing-board nirvana, while their reggae counterparts, creating under
the spell of Vick's NyQuil (a religious sacrament in Rastafarian culture),
settled into a steady, metronomic groove, with the settling part every
bit as crucial as the grooving. It was just like golf, except no one
seemed to be moving.

Funk was first popularized in 1895 with the dynamic debut of
Funk & Wagnalls dictionary, but within the world of pop music it's one

of the many godsons (along with disco, hip-hop, and death-defying joyrides) of James Brown. In early funk songs like "Cold Sweat" (1967) and "Sex Machine" (1970), Brown virtually abandoned melody altogether for a new rhythm-based style of music with a peculiar code of language (a series of grunts, coughs, and hiccups, with lots of "Yeeeeeowws!" tossed in for good measure) that not even Rich Little could properly duplicate. Although Brown was the primary architect of funk, the contribution of another James, the James Gang, shouldn't be underestimated — their "Funk #49" (1970) converted thousands to this vibrant new musical form. Two groups that latched onto the Gang's minimalist experiments early were Kool and the Gang (obvious homage) and B.T. Express, who hit the charts in 1974 with "Jungle Boogie" and "Do It ('Til You're Satisfied)," respectively. Both songs had insistent beats, sneaky bass patterns, chanted vocals, and both repeated their titles about a thousand times, leading to their immediate adoption by progressive learning institutions as after-school detention sing-alongs.

The real funk breakthrough of the 1970s was masterminded by two men locked in a rivalry as bitter as Muhammed Ali vs. Joe Frazier, perhaps even Bo Donaldson vs. Terry Jacks. In one corner was George Clinton, great-great grandson of America's fourth Vice-President and the flamboyant Mother Hubbard figure behind the extended P-Funk nexus (Parliament, Funkadelic, Bootsy's Rubber Band, Parlet, the Brides of Funkenstein, the Step-parents of Funkenstein, Sgt. Funkenstein's Lonely Hearts Rubber Band, etc.). In the opposite corner sat Maurice White, the Arthur Godfrey of seventies dance music and spiritual advisor to the mammoth Earth, Wind & Fire plexus (Earth, Wind & Fire, the Emotions). Actually, Clinton and White had a lot in common: both peddled eccentric ideas (Clinton's satirical digs at the distressing state of black music and the even more distressing sight of white people dancing to it, White's corny metaphysical musings); both donned outrageous get-ups (Clinton's Marlene Dietrich frightwig, White's Ancient Egyptian duds); and both conducted arena tours in the late seventies preposterous enough to make even Pink Floyd envious (Parliament landing on stage in the mother of all motherships, EWF hovering over crowds with their instruments in hand). Pink Floyd's Roger Waters was so impressed he briefly considered a group name change to Here Come the Brides of P-Floyd.

Where George and Maurice differed was in their approach to funk. P-Funk albums veered off in so many different directions — acid rock, psychedelia, be-bop, nursery rhymes, Gregorian chants, Appalachian folk music — they often ended up in that esoteric kingdom called nowhere. Those that were released under the Funkadelic name were characterized by an overload of Hendrixian guitars (1971's *Maggot Brain* and 1973's *Cosmic Slop*), while Parliament albums were loopier, Sly Stone-influenced trumpet-and-keyboard exercises. Clinton built up a loyal following throughout the decade, but he only managed to break into the Top Forty on pop charts three times: Parliament's "Tear the Roof Off the Sucker" (1976) and "Flash Light" (1978), both big disco hits, and Funkadelic's "One Nation Under a Groove" (1978), one of the few P-Funk creations you could dance and hum along to at the same time. Perhaps George's truest legacy was his appealingly infantile character studies: Dr. Funkenstein, Star Child, Sir Nose D'Voidoffunk, and Mr. Wiggles would have all made A-1 Saturday morning cartoons. But then, so would have a lot of folks in this book.

Earth, Wind & Fire's auto-pilot funk was the inverse of P-Funk's short-circuited bumper-car version. Although EWF had a tendency to 'stretch out' and show off their Spyro Gyra wizardry on LPs, they managed to keep their musical wits about them when it came to singles. In all, they made fourteen trips to the Top Forty in the seventies, every one as polished as Steely Dan yet as chewy-chewy as ELO. "Shining Star " (1975), "Serpentine Fire" (1977), and "September" (1978) were filled with so many percolating bongo patterns and intricate horn charts, listeners could ignore their built-in self-enlightenment programs and dance the King Tut until all hours of the morning. EWF's name said it all: 'Earth' because they were of the common man; 'Wind' because they blew mercurially; and 'Fire' because they went through many session musicians before Maurice got the precise sound he wanted.

While Clinton and White battled it out centre-stage, several funk supporting players snuck onto the charts in their wake. Most prominent was the Commodores, who first hit in 1974 with "Machine Gun," a hokey synth-instrumental imitated shamelessly within a matter of months by Mike Post's "Rockford Files" theme. After that they vacillated between the harder funk of 1977's "Brick House" (later commemorated in Tom Wolfe's *From Bauhaus to Brick House*), and ballads like "Easy" and the count-along favorite "Three Times a Lady" (1978), where lead singer Lionel Richie unleashed the rampaging Dan Fogelberg hidden inside his closet. Representing funk's nastier side was the Ohio Players, who went to number one twice: "Fire" (1974), led off by the same siren that Paper Lace used on "The Night Chicago Died" only five months earlier,[1] and "Love Rollercoaster" (1975), which was powered by the most nasal vocal this side of Lily Tomlin's telephone operator, Ernestine. Errol Brown, lead singer for Britain's Hot Chocolate, also displayed sinus problems on "You Sexy Thing" (1975) and "Every 1's a Winner" (1978), and he remains the decade's fourth most important bald man behind Telly Savalas, Isaac Hayes, and aging chrome-dome Charlie Brown. The Brothers Johnson served up the lightest funk on the planet with "Strawberry Letter 23" (1977), which combined Genesis at their most sheepish — its guitar solo came right out of "The Lamb Lies Down on Broadway"— and Temptations-style harmonies. The best female funk of the decade was provided by the criminally voluptuous Chaka Khan, who led her band Rufus into the Top Ten three times, most memorably on the Stevie Wonder composition "Tell Me Something Good" (1974). OK, we will — we're going to spare you any discussion of Latimore, the Gap Band, L.T.D., Maze, Slave, or Thelonius Funk.

If, at times, even the best funk artists threatened to lull half their audience to sleep, reggae initially seemed like the aural equivalent of hypnosis. Such impressions, however, were largely a matter of perspective. In Jamaica, where reggae originated, it served as the soundtrack to a tense political climate. In England, reggae was a profound inspiration to punk rockers. Here in North America, inspired by innovators like Bobby Bloom ("Montego Bay") and the Guess Who ("Follow Your Daughter Home," 1973), reggae was a kindred spirit to Fleetwood Mac and Pablo Cruise — perfect beach-volleyball music.[2]

[1] Roxy Music would eventually base an entire album on this amazing coincidence.

[2] If you need some proof, check out "Hotel California" and Bo Derek's cornrows in the movie *10* (1979).

Reggae's leading light was Bob Marley, who first gained notice on these shores in 1972 when he and his band the Wailers (with Bunny Wailer and Peter Tosh) released *Catch a Fire*. At a time when reggae needed a foothold in North America, *Catch a Fire*'s ribald skirt-chasing episodes ("Kinky Reggae") and revolution-in-the-streets stuff ("Concrete Jungle") went down as easy as the Beach Boys' "Catch a Wave." The Wailers next release, *Burnin'* (1973), was equally impressive, though more militant overall. Its most popular cut, "I Shot the Sheriff" (later taken to number one by Eric Clapton), pitted barber Floyd Lawson against Sheriff Andy Griffith, with Floyd insisting that he did not shoot the Deputy Barney Fife. After *Burnin'*, Bob, Bunny, and Peter went their separate ways: Peter devoted his time to fighting for the legalization of sunflower seeds, Bunny moved to Liverpool and started a psychedelic band called Bunny and the Echomen, and Bob begrudgingly cashed in on his 'King of Reggae' title with a series of B-movies that included *Jailhouse Dub* and *Viva Kingston!* Meanwhile, some near-hits edged Bob closer and closer to North American superstardom: "Jamming" (1977) had Marley repeating "we're jamming" eight times in a row really fast without once swallowing his tongue (he didn't fare nearly as well on its follow-up, "Toy Boat"), while "No Woman No Cry" and "Is This Love" (1978) were West Coast enough to suggest that he was listening to Doobies as well as smoking them.

Marley towered over the entire reggae genre like a Jolly Ganja Giant, but a few other performers made their own claims to immortality. Jimmy Cliff was acclaimed by film critics for his portrayal of Ivan, a serenading gangster in Perry Henzell's *The Harder They Come* (1972), and on the soundtrack's opening cut, "You Can Get It If You Really Want," he came up with the *I'm OK, You're OK* of Jamaican pop. 'Tootsie Pop' Hibbert, lead singer for the Maytals, had a gruff voice that earned him favorable comparisons to Otis Redding, but he was also an unabashed John Denver fan, as the group's beautiful version of "Country Roads" (1973) made clear. (John returned the favor with a dynamite gospel-folk rendition of "Funky Kingston" the following year.)

Burning Spear was the most combatant and mesmerizing of reggae bands, a devastating mixture on *Marcus Garvey* and its instrumental 'dub' version, *Garvey's Ghost* (both 1976). Not to be outdone, white funk-reggae band and avid baseball fans Wild Cherry ("Play That Funky Music," 1976) added a strange twist to Spear's twin-set when they released *Steve Garvey* and *Garvey's Glove* to universal fanfare a few months later.

Funk and reggae might have appeared to arrive from two different planets to innocent bystanders — different song tempos, different lyrical concerns, different hairdos — but, as one man proved, it didn't matter if you were black, white, turquoise, or even if you couldn't tell the difference, so long as you had a vision. Enter again Stevie Wonder, who joined American funk and Caribbean rhythms in holy matrimony (with jazz, gospel, and art rock invited to the reception) on his 1976 double-opus, *Songs in the Key of Life*. Stevie had been heading towards a major artistic statement ever since he dropped the 'Little' from his name, got his own mailbox at Motown, and purchased his first Gentle Giant record. Picking up where *Innervisions* (1973) and *Fulfillingness' First Finale* (1974) left off, *Songs* was a major piece of work on several levels: a lively dance record, a bedtime companion to *Sweet Baby James* (J.T. was even acknowledged in the credits alongside such heroes to black America as Carole King and Jeff Beck), an astonishing display of multi-tracking and Moog doodling (aka 'moogling'), and the most phenomenally popular record of its day. The album generated two number-one singles, "I Wish" and "Sir Duke," the latter a jazzy tribute to Ellington, Gene Chandler, John Wayne, George Duke, and Sir Lord Baltimore.

Songs in the Key of Life was a brilliant, pretentious, fun, and boring work of artistry (sometimes within the same song), and as such was a fitting summation to black pop in the mid-seventies. It is with great regret that we must forego any detailed analysis of Stevie's remarkable follow-up to *Songs*, 1979's *Journey Through the Secret Life of Robert Plant*, in order that we may proceed immediately to the not-so-secret life of another major contributor to the development of black music in the late seventies.

Chapter 20

THINK OF ME AND TRY NOT TO LAUGH

"You know who else I listen to all the time, you're not going to believe this — Al Jolson. He was a great entertainer. I only wish I could be as good as he was. But of course, it's hard."
— Rod Stewart, 1974.

IT'S been said that Brits are incapable of producing rock and roll without irony or posturing. Obviously, every righteous British roots band from Freddie and the Dreamers to Frankie Goes to Hollywood has proven this heinous charge to be completely unfounded, but there's no getting around the fact that enterprising Englishmen can play rock *stars* better than just about anyone around. Nowhere is this more evident than in the career of Rod Stewart. One of the most critically acclaimed and popular artists of the early seventies, Stewart pulled a Mr. Hyde practically overnight in the middle part of the decade, settling down in Hollywood to churn out a brand of glamorous pop that epitomized whatever it was about the seventies that just made people's flesh crawl. Had he simply assumed his place in Tinseltown from the beginning, nobody would have batted an eye. What was at issue was that Rod had traveled from point A ("Maggie May," British Dylan, tartan trousers, 'umble soccer fanatic) to point Z (Hef's mansion, "Da Ya Think I'm Sexy," Deney Terrio wardrobe, ubiquitous what-me-worry grin) with no demonstrable sense of guilt, thus placing him near the top of many lists of evil seventies people; nudged out of number one by Idi Amin, he leapfrogged over Richard Nixon, Son of Sam, and those goofy Hagar Brothers from *Hee Haw.*

Stewart stepped into the 1970s with *Gasoline Alley* (1970), the title track of which embodied the decade's first and most affecting version of Rod: a singer with a unique rasp, lyrics that poignantly reflected on days gone by, and a mandolin player who ran amok. Rod's next LP, *Every Picture Tells a Story* (1971), was even better: a great statement of affirmation when the sixties hangover heard on *Exile* and Ringo's *Beaucoup of Blues* still held sway, bringing a singer-songwriter's touch to music that actually sounded like rock and roll. Everyone loves "Maggie May," the title track was hilarious, and "Mandolin Wind" influenced artists ranging from Dylan ("Idiot Wind") to Kansas ("Dust in the Wind") to Mocedades ("Eres Tu"). *Never a Dull Moment* (1972) followed, which technically had a couple but also included "You Wear It Well," the most rustic-sounding record ever to name-drop Jackie Onassis (Diane von Furstenberg had too many syllables) and a foreshadowing of the direction in which Rod the social butterfly was headed.

The next couple years were mostly uneventful, marked by solo outings that tried (but didn't manage) to capture the good humor of *Every Picture*, along with some recordings done with the Faces. The best of these legendary slopfests was "Stay With Me" (1972), Rod and Company's thoughtful contribution to an emerging feminist con-sciousness: "In the morning, please don't say you love me/'Cause I'll only kick you out of the door!" Gloria Steinem and Germaine Greer were deeply impressed.

Part two of the Rod Stewart story begins in 1975 with the release of *Atlantic Crossing.* Yes, Rod had crossed the Atlantic to evade the taxman and put an end to his cross-continental shopping expeditions, but in the eyes of his soon-to-be detractors he had also crossed the lines of good taste. The musical emphasis shifted from album tracks to singles, and Rod's rock and roll backup band was replaced by anonymous studio pros (maybe even a few of those handymen from Toto, who jammed with everyone from Bryan Ferry to the Dead Boys). To top it all off, there was his well-publicized affair

125

with Britt Ekland. Who in their right mind, everyone agreed, would go out with a gorgeous Swedish actress? Universal disgust multiplied at a rate only exceeded by Rod's record sales, and *Atlantic Crossing* joined *Jaws* as 1975's most controversial seafaring epic.

Although *Atlantic Crossing* contained a couple of minor singles ("This Old Heart of Mine" and "Sailing"), it wasn't until *A Night on the Town* (1976) that Rod's flood of hits began in earnest. The album's cover featured him holding a champagne glass and staring vacantly into the camera, one of the era's key images and the inspiration for Richard Hell's punk anthem "Blank Generation" a year later. For the rest of the decade, Rod's hits ranged from fluky works of ballad genius (1977's double-sided "The First Cut Is the Deepest"/"I Don't Want To Talk About It," which kept the Sex Pistols' "God Save the Queen" out of the number-one spot in England) to El Mocambo-era Stones ("Hot Legs," 1978) to coy mea culpas ("I Was Only Joking," 1978). All of them were as likeable as they were ridiculous — a good combination then, a good combination today, a good combination tomorrow.

Two number-ones defined the era for Rod, "Tonight's the Night" (1976) and "Da Ya Think I'm Sexy?" (1978). "Tonight's the Night" was a classic tale of seduction, as sexy as the Shirelles song of the same name ("Spread your wings and let me come inside," cooed Rod) and possibly, just possibly, sexier than the Neil Young LP of the same name. "Da Ya Think I'm Sexy," on the other hand, combined a sumptuous disco track with one of those great Euro-Fiddler-on-the-Roof hooks so prevalent at the time (Donna Summer's "Hot Stuff," Boney M's "Rasputin"). Even though 'Rod Stewart' and 'disco' were by now constant objects of derision, you could nevertheless hear a trillion females from Omaha to Tokyo chant, "Ya, we da think ya is sexy!"

With that all-out fearless jump into disco, Rod celebrated the end of the decade with at least as much verve as he had welcomed its arrival. His critics continued to multiply in direct proportion to his ever-zealous fan base, and Rod-bashing became standard behavior for critics, trashophobics, and high school wiseacres alike. It's now apparent, however, that Mr. Hyde was at least as much fun as Dr. Jekyll, and if you don't believe us, blindfold yourself and play "Maggie May" in tandem with "The First Cut Is the Deepest" sometime and see which you prefer. Something tells us it'll be a toss-up, especially if you cross your fingers and stand on your head while doing it.

Chapter 21

Fun, Fun, Fun on the Autobahn

"I have no pretensions to Bruce's throne. I have no arguments
with Bruce, but we get pitted against each other, right? I know
if I sat down with Bruce and talked to him head to head, it would
be like, 'Yeah, let's go have a hot dog.' "
— Billy Joel, 1980.

As the late seventies approached, bringing punk and disco and
lots of name-calling to the world of pop, fans of 'no frills' rock needed
some new heroes to step forward and carry the news. Luckily, there
were three pop-rock everymen who seemed made to order, three
guys who symbolically took a stand against late-seventies hype in
much the same way that HRS had squared off against glitter and Paper
Lace earlier in the decade. We're referring to Bruce Springsteen, Bob
Seger, and Billy Joel, a trio of pre-punks for disenfranchised Bud
drinkers which collectively embarked on a nostalgic anti-crusade for
a more conscientious work ethic among rock stars, a return to solid
blue-collar values, and more of those cool teenage rumbles like they
used to have in *West Side Story*. The three of them heroically bridged
the gap between Gilbert O'Sullivan and the Clash: one minute they
could be quiet and introspective, while the next they'd be gritting their
teeth and raising their fists against one act of human malevolence or

another. The three B's weren't completely above a little show business themselves — visions come back of Bruce bringing out a stretcher for encores, Bob's flying saxophonist, and Billy setting fire to his Steinway — but that's not what people loved about them. They were, in a much larger sense, armed and ready to do battle with the Village People and the Knack on behalf of distraught and confused rock fans the world over. And then, if all went well, they'd get together and go have a hot dog.

Bruce Springsteen, who loomed largest of the three, first gained attention in the early seventies as one in a long succession of 'new Dylans' then flooding the market. The comparison rested on a number of remarkable similarities between the two men: both were discovered by John Hammond and signed to Columbia Records; both had a penchant for melodramatic mini-street operas populated by various gypsies, tramps, and thieves; both mumbled habitually; both groomed themselves not so habitually; both were world-class pinochle players; neither had ever been to the South Pole.

Springsteen's first two albums, *Greetings from Asbury Park, N.J.* and *The Wild, the Innocent, and the E Street Shuffle* (both 1973), didn't sell much, but he and the E Street Band gained attention on the live circuit for long-winded gigs that lasted 9, 10, 11 hours, or at least until the last janitor left the building urging Bruce to "lock up when you're finished." After witnessing one of these marathon sessions in a Boston bar in 1974, world-famous psychic Jeanne Dixon irrevocably changed the course of history with a single sentence: "I saw rock and roll future," Jeanne wrote in Boston's *Real Paper*, "and its name is Bruce Springsteen." CBS records splashed her words across newspapers and magazines throughout the country, and Bruce's next LP, *Born to Run*, became the breakthrough he had been waitng for.

Born to Run's title track, one of the most famous songs of the seventies, crammed in every epic romantic symbol imaginable: cars, girls, streets, cops, tires, stop signs, mufflers, crosswalks, parking tickets, first love, floormats, parents, windshield wipers, shock absorbers, and more streets. Elsewhere, "Thunder Road" quoted Roy Orbison, "She's the One" harkened back to the Crystals, and "Tenth Avenue Freeze-Out" resembled Sam & Dave; apparently no one seemed to mind that the future of rock and roll hadn't purchased a record in over ten years. To cap off a screwy year, October 1975 saw

Springsteen land on the covers of *Time* and *Newsweek* simultaneously, with the latter calling its article "The Making of a Rock Star." That same month, *Family Circle* published its controversial "The Making of a Spinach Soufflé"; the synchronicity of events was astounding.

Because of a lawsuit with his manager, Mike 'One Bad' Appel, Springsteen had to wait three years to release his next LP, *Darkness on the Edge of Town* (1978). During this layoff period, a new class of scruffier-than-thou 'new Springsteens' had emerged — Steve Forbert, Steve Gibbons, Dwight Twilley, Little Johnny Cougar — leaving Bruce no longer such an anomaly in the pop world. *Darkness* was a big success anyway, and it broke important new ground by expanding Bruce's horizons well beyond cars to include trucks, vans, and Winnebagos. The album's best tracks were "Badlands," "Candy's Room," and "The Promised Land," the latter a direct response to the threat posed by new wave and disco: "Mr., I ain't the Cars or Boney M/And I believe in the promised land."

Springsteen's struggle to reach the top looked easy next to Bob Seger's. A spare part who fell off an auto assembly line, Seger had been releasing records since the late sixties, hitting once with "Ramblin' Gamblin' Man" (1968) and then disappearing from public view (unless you lived in Detroit, where he was surpassed only by Bo Schembecler as a living legend). The early Seger style was as rah-rah as Springsteen's, though Bob leaned more toward the Rolling Stones and fifties rock and roll. "Katmandu," a local smash from 1975, was prototypical Bob: a simple blues progression, a shrieking sax, and lots of frantic huffing and puffing from Seger. Diehard fans considered it the second coming of Little Richard, while Detroit disc jockeys appreciated the perfect segue it made into Pratt & McClain's "Happy Days" theme.

As Seger found himself approaching middle age with only one national hit to his name, he decided to do what all critically endangered rock folk did in the seventies: he released a double-live set, 1976's *Live Bullet* , a giant thank-you card to the thousands who had stuck with him over the years. "Can we rock and roll ya one more?" Bob cajoled the *Live Bullet* audience; "No Bob, that just won't do, please rock and roll us *two* more!" the audience roared back. *Live*

Bullet was merely a warm-up for *Night Moves*, one of 1976's biggest selling and most acclaimed albums. The title song, a relaxed evocation of what it was like to be young and in love and groping like wild beasts in the back seat of a car, was rock music's answer to both *The Summer of '42* and Frank Sinatra's "It Was a Very Good Year," elevating bathetic sentimentality to bittersweet grandeur. "Rock 'n' Roll Never Forgets," which made deferential mention of "all Chuck's children," inspired much swooning also, a lovely tribute to Chuck Mangione and how much he meant to the rich history of instrumental rock.

The true essence of Bobdom was "Old Time Rock 'n' Roll" (which never forgets, by the way), a single taken from *Stranger in Town* (1978). The song caught Bob reminiscing about "the days of old" and bemoaning the proliferation of disco (he'd "rather hear some blues or funky old soul"), and as if that wasn't enough to make him the Dwight D. Eisenhower of rock and soul, he later refused to take part in the early-eighties Batcave craze as well ("Nothing personal," shrugged Bob, "just not my thing"). Despite only middling chart success, "Old Time Rock 'n' Roll" became Seger's trademark song, helped in large measure by its status as a wedding-reception/ bar-mitzvah/monster-truck-rally classic.

In a decidedly poppier vein than Bruce or Bob was Billy Joel, the one bonafide singles artist of the three and America's answer to Elton John. Initially, Joel was lumped alongside Springsteen in the 'new Dylan' category thanks to his first hit "Piano Man" (1973), aka "The Lonesome Life of Hoagy Carmichael." The song was an ambitious one, a six-minute meditation on what it was like to toil away anonymously for unappreciative and incomprehending audiences within the vast motel heartland of America. Next to Billy, later imitations like *Fernwood 2-Night*'s Tony Roletti and Bill Murray's "Star Wars Medley" barely scratched the surface of the piano-man experience. Much to Joel's credit he didn't always aim so high, paying heed to some childhood words of wisdom from his grandmother —"Billy," she gently whispered in his ear, "don't be a hero."

"Piano Man" didn't automatically propel Billy to stardom, but 1977's *The Stranger* (heavy Camus influence) unleashed a number of hits that today are touchstones of Adult Contemporary playlists: "Just the Way You Are," a syrupy ode to an average plain-Jane (someone like Christie Brinkley, perhaps, whom Billy later married); "Movin' Out (Anthony's Song)," where Billy's delivery of "heart a-ta-ta-ta-ta-ta-tack" perfectly captured the texture and ambience of mafioso gunfire; and "Only the Good Die Young," which terrorized papal authority by declaring "sinners are much more fun" (with Billy's sadistic cackling throughout making even a few pagans sit up and take notice). Joel waved goodbye to the seventies with "Big Shot", first in a series of singles (1980's "You May Be Right" and "It's Still Rock and Roll to Me") that proved he could kick out at least as many jams as the Fabulous Poodles, Moon Martin, or the Incredible Shrinking Dickies.

By the end of the seventies, the Village People and the Knack were no longer a threat — the gauntlet had been laid down, and Bruce, Bob, and Billy picked it up and wrestled it to the ground. The eighties presented the three B's with challenges even more formidable, but once again they dug in their heels for a long, uncertain fight against Wang Chung, Europe, and Matt Bianco.

Chapter 22

A Thousand Points of Light

"Encore. The new Argent album that's larger than live. About the
only place a band can really stretch out these days is on stage. And
nobody knows it — or plays it — better than Argent."
— Epic Records ad copy, 1975.

It's time now to pay proper tribute to what you may have
noticed is an expanding subplot in our story, a shadowy history of
seventies pop music with a life of its own, an opportunistic virus
infecting virtually everyone who passes before our eyes. We're not
talking about bad haircuts, although they were a serious problem too.
Rather, it was the ubiquitous live album that housed the seventies'
deepest secrets, most profound intrigues, and biggest horselaughs,
combining commerce, expedience, volume, inanity, bombast, pre-
dictability, self-indulgence, and a limitless supply of hokey titles into
handy little packages of portable me-decade home entertainment.
Because people had little to say to one another in the seventies
anyway, it made perfect sense that pop music should be overtaken by
the idea that concerts were best appreciated in the safety of one's
own living room, staring intently at an elaborate network of Marantz
speakers, grooving and communing with God, nature, and Foghat,
and trying to catch the 'vibe' that would transport one through time

and space to the seventeenth row of Detroit's Cobo Hall. From *Woodstock* (1970) to Seger's *Live Bullet (1976)* to Neil Young's *Live Rust* (1979), that was how dedicated fans of live music got their fix. Who those people were who attended the actual concerts in the first place, nobody really knows.

To understand how absolutely central live albums were to the 1970s, how abundant they were and how automatic a part of anyone's career they became, it's best to ignore for a moment the decade's biggest names (all of whom could be reasonably expected to take advantage of the low-risk proposition a live LP represented), and instead rummage through the debris left behind by those whose aspirations were only exceeded by their presumptuousness. To wit: the Three Degrees made a live album. Be Bop Deluxe made a live album. Tower of Power, Pure Prairie League, and the Climax Blues Band made live albums. Hot Tuna and Helen Reddy made live albums, and so did Don McLean, Renaissance, Wet Willie, Buddy Miles, Kansas, Focus, Curved Air, Jo Jo Gunne, the New Riders of the Purple Sage, the Village People, Loggins & Messina, Hawkwind, It's a Beautiful Day, Poco, David Cassidy, and Amon Duul II. *Who on earth was Amon Duul II?* Good question, but like everyone else they did manage to get a live album out in the seventies — everybody except Leadbelly did, and the only thing that stopped him was the handicap of being dead. Oddly enough, the Rolling Stones released a couple anyway.

Live albums came in a variety of sizes: there were single-LP releases (the Who's *Live at Leeds*, 1970; Lou Reed's *Rock n Roll Animal*, 1974), three-LP gatefolds (*Wings Over America*, 1976), four-LP boxes (*Chicago at Carnegie Hall*, 1971), and thirteen-LP super-colliders (*Yes, That's Right, Time for Another Live Album from the Grateful Dead*, 1970-79). The most common format, however, was the sacred 'double-live.' It didn't matter whether the artist in question had fifteen years of material from which to draw (James Brown's *Sex Machine*, 1970), ten years (David Bowie's *Stage*, 1978), or only three or four albums (Donna Summer's *Live and More*, 1978), there was always a way to reconfigure a career into a double-live. In short, all one had to do was 'stretch out' a little, put the Pinocchio Principle into play, and double-lives started falling from trees. With this strategy in effect,

133

three-minute songs became five-minute work-outs, five-minute work-outs got a coda and became eight-minute journeys, eight-minute journeys got a coda, a prologue, and a drum solo and became fifteen-minute epics, and fifteen-minute epics got a libretto, an orchestra, a few footnotes, a map, and some lovely parting gifts and became full-blown thirty-minute dissertations. You can imagine what stretching out entailed on LPs like Gentle Giant's *Playing the Fool* (1976), Tangerine Dream's *Ricochet* (1976), and ELP's *Welcome Back My Friends to the Show That Never Ends* (1974). Actually, you don't have to imagine, that last title says it all — Keith Emerson's still in the middle of his clavichord solo.

Another means of artificial inflation employed on live albums was to jabber away extemporaneously about anything and everything — before songs, between songs, during songs, or instead do what Lou Reed did on *Take No Prisoners* (1978), which was to squeeze in bits and parts of songs between all the jabbering. 'Stage patter' it's called, and it was the secret weapon of all live albums, a chance for fans to hear their favorite performers speak their minds and share all their good cheer and wisdom that never made it into song (provided, of course, it wasn't Jean-Luc Ponty, Itzhak Perlman, or some other highbrow show-off who just stood on stage and played). The guys in King Crimson cracking jokes, touching anecdotes from Gary Gliiter's childhood, and thunderous rock and roll battle cries from Geddy Lee were the real reasons why people happily handed over money for bad versions of songs they already owned twice over. Although there's some room for argument, our choices for the decade's three wildest patter-platters are Kiss' *Alive!*, the Stooges' *Metallic K.O.* (1976), and Ted Nugent's *Double-Live Gonzo!* (1978). Most of the latter two is unquotable in a family book like this one, but the first offers a dazzling array of "alright"s, "rock 'n' roll"s, and "dynamite"s, plus Paul Stanley conducting a rigorously scientific audience survey, almost as if he were in the Gallup organization.

Here are some other treasured snippets of pitter-patter:

—"Are you ready Dallas? Are you ready to dance and boogie-woogie?" (Asleep at the Wheel's *Served Live* , 1979).

—"All right, gonna give you some brain salad surgery!" (ELP, *Welcome Back*).

—"How many people out there read *Kerrang? ... KERRANG?...* Nobody? Anyhow ..."* (Thor's *Live in Detroit* , 1978).

—"We need a bouncer for table number six over here, these guys are getting a little rowdy." (Pablo Cruise's *Live at the El Mocambo,* 1979).

Inspirational beyond words — can you imagine how frightened those people at the El Mocambo must have been, how calming an effect the Cruisers' peace negotiations must have had?

There was no better measure of the live album's mystique in the 1970s than the improbable case of *Frampton Comes Alive!* (1976). To this day, the sudden ascension of British guitarist Peter Frampton from an unheralded eighth-banana to owner of the then-biggest-selling LP of all time remains one of the most remarkable turnabouts in pop music history. In 1974, Frampton was all but unknown to anyone not on the mailing list of *Guitar Player* magazine. He had done time in the Herd, Humble Pie, and his own band Frampton's Camel, but the average rock fan still got him confused with Australian golfer Bruce Crampton and legendary vibeologist Lionel Hampton. With that stellar background behind him, Peter naturally felt the time was right for a double-live; within a year, *Frampton Comes Alive!* topped *Billboard* , broke three hit singles ("Show Me the Way," "Baby, I Love Your Way," and "Baby, I'd Love for You To Show Me Your Way"), and sold somewhere in the neighborhood of eight million copies. It was Frampton madness everywhere, the dawning of a Frampton frontier, Frampton in the morning, noon, and night. Has anyone ever figured out what happened? Judging from the glazed expression Peter wore on the album's jacket, he didn't understand this or any other of life's great mysteries either.

Peter quickly fizzled, but live albums just kept on coming and coming for the rest of the decade. The gap between what they were supposed to be (documents, souvenirs, bargains, career overviews, serendipitous Christmas gifts) and what they actually were (okay to scratch, maul, and spill stuff on because it all sounded like crowd noise anyway) bothered no one. Live albums never went away, of course, but there are far fewer of them nowadays. Box sets have taken their place: in the seventies Uriah Heep got a live album (1973's *Live*), but in 1997 they'll be the subject of a box set, *Heap O' Heep* or something to that effect. It won't be the same enchanting experience, though. When fans lay back and close their eyes during *Heap O' Heep*'s rare studio master of "Easy Livin'," they won't be able to feel the Marshalls down to their marrow, sense the roadies waiting in the wings, or conjure up in their imaginations a sea of Bics pointed heavenward. Worst of all, the box set won't talk back.

Chapter 23

AL STEWART EXPLORES YOUR MIND

"There's a thin line between what's hip and what's unhip. I like
to walk that line".
— Stephen Bishop, 1978.

IN *The Book of Lists*, a reference volume published in 1977,
there's a role call of the ten most beautiful words in the English
language as selected by linguist Wilfred J. Funk: 'golden,' 'lullaby,'
'melody,' 'chimes,' 'dawn,' 'tranquil,' 'mist,' 'hush,' 'murmuring,' and
'luminous.' Clearly W.J. was not a man who collected TV-advertised
albums during the seventies, or he surely would have added an
eleventh: 'Ronco.' Say it a few times yourself and see how gently it
rolls off the tongue — peaceful, delicate, evocative, it's a word that
summons forth memories of dewy spring mornings and crisp autumn
sunsets.

Ronco Teleproducts Inc., an Illinois-based company that wrested
control of the late-seventies TV album market from K-Tel International, gave shape and substance to the decade's waning years just
as K-Tel had done in the early seventies. With 'good taste' becoming
an increasingly abstract concept as the decade progressed, Ronco
even managed to bestow upon its forerunner a retroactive veneer of
sobriety and elegance: next to a Ronco album, K-Tel product began

to look as if it had been released under the auspices of Deutsche Grammophon. K-Tel was cheesy, but Ronco was the whole cow-and-a-half. Among its most unforgettable collections were *Let's Party* (1978), which was decorated with an uncorked champagne bottle spewing a jet stream of bubbly; *Boogie Nights*, also from 1978, where you were confronted by a neon marquee on which a pair of lonely paper cutouts did an existential dance of death; and *Super Sonic*, a 1979 release featuring a gigantic pair of flying headphones on the cover, surrounded on all sides by winged LPs and woolly cumulus clouds.

Ronco collections invariably concentrated on the disco music that dominated Top Forty radio in the late seventies, but because there is a full discussion of disco later in this book, we'll instead examine Ronco as a K-Tel-styled clearing house for all the non-disco fungi that managed to find a niche on singles charts of the day. Probably the biggest star of the Ronco years, the Ronco career to rival Cher's K-Tel career, was the Steve Miller Band, who in the mid-seventies ran off a string of post-"Beach Baby" anthems that unleashed the repressed nice-guy hidden deep in the heart of seventies solipsism and egomania. It became hard for a while to differentiate Steve's crew from an unstoppable singles machine of a previous era, the Glenn Miller Orchestra. Both men left behind formal roots (blues for Steve, jazz for Glenn) to achieve massive popularity; Steve's "Take the Money and Run" and "Rock'n Me" (both 1976) were as riff-primal and fearless as Glenn's "In the Mood"; Steve gave us "Swingtown" (1977), Glenn helped invent 'swing'; Steve sang about birds ("Fly Like an Eagle," 1976), so did Glenn (swallows and nightingales); Steve flew airplanes ("Jet Airliner," 1977), Glenn crashed in one; Steve celebrated sex in the Amazon ("Jungle Love," 1977), Glenn often performed wearing a tuxedo. Quite uncanny, really, and there were some astounding similarities between Steve and Mitch Miller, too.

Tuxedos were the calling card of another Ronco icon, the thoroughly overcooked Meat Loaf, though with Loaf it was less a case of wearing something than inflating it with helium and pressure-sucking himself inside. Meat's *Bat Out of Hell* remains one of the decade's most emblematic warehouse blowouts: a conflation of heavy metal witchcraft, HRS calorie count, numbing Todd Rundgren production, a runaway verbosity straight out of *Born to Run*, delirious art-rock theatrics, and poignant Morris Albert balladry, all of it charged with a sense of style and purpose that belonged completely to Ronco. The LP's key song was "Paradise By the Dashboard Light," which picked up where Bob Seger left off and turned teenage groping (front seat this time) into an extended baseball metaphor. Play-by-play was handled by Phil Rizzuto, and there were even breaks for hot dogs and pizza after the second, third, fifth, and eighth innings.

Body doubles were common inside the Ronco universe: either Loaf or Eddie Money for Bruce Springsteen, Leo Sayer for Elton John, Eric Carmen for Paul McCartney, Bonnie Tyler for Rod Stewart, the Little River Band for Pablo Cruise, an endless supply of pinch-hitters able to extract the essence of the originals and reinvigorate it with a touch of Ronco élan. Eddie Money was famous for being pop music's first prominent ex-cop, an apprenticeship that came through vividly in his tales of high-speed car chases ("Baby Hold On," 1978) and metered-parking violations ("Two Tickets to Paradise," 1978). No one caught the spirit of 1977 better than Leo Sayer, who twice reached number one that year with "You Make Me Feel Like Dancing" and "When I Need You." Time was when Leo gave concerts dressed as a clown, but no way anyone was laughing at him now. Eric Carmen had left the Raspberries in 1974 to pursue a solo career, but out on his own he still found himself tormented by an unfulfilled quest for complete solitude. As far as Eric was concerned, "All By Myself" (1975) and "Never Gonna Fall in Love Again" (1976) made it clear that hell would always be other people. Bonnie Tyler's "It's a Heartache" (1978) was no less morbid, possibly because she still mourned the loss of her throat nodules in a 1976 operation, which explained her Stewart-like rasp —"It's a Sore Throat" wouldn't have sold anything, so Bonnie's invocation of poetic license was more than justified. Australia's Little River Band, a perennial chart favorite in the late seventies, extended a transcontinental hand of friendship on "Help Is On Its Way" (1977), exuded joyous nostalgia on "Happy Anniversary" (1977) and "Reminiscing" (1978), and plunged headlong into the dizzying romantic swirl of "Lady" (1979).

Coming out of Britain, meanwhile, Al Stewart's "Year of the Cat" (1976) and Gerry Rafferty's "Baker Street" (1978) were high-fidelity folk standards of the first order. Al's had something to do with Humphrey Bogart, or Peter Lorre, or maybe it was Peter Criss, while Gerry, who had earlier been one half of Stealers Wheel on "Stuck In the Middle With You" (1973), had the great honor of bridging the K-Tel and Ronco eras in a single body. No less evocative was Gary Wright, a part-British (former member of Spooky Tooth), part-American (born in New Jersey), all-Ronco keyboard demon who earned consecutive number-two hits in 1976 with "Dream Weaver" and "Love Is Alive." The cover of the *Dream Weaver* album, a shot of Gary with his eyes closed and his scarf blowing freely, more or less captured what he was all about.

One of Ronco's greatest glories was a small group of male troubadours who exploded the deep-rooted melancholy so common in the margins of late-seventies pop. The names Stephen Bishop, Andrew Gold, Robert John, and Rupert Holmes still resonate with the sighs and daydreams of those who were shut out from the punk-disco free-for-all, victims of the wholesale abandonment of a lost demi-generation. Stephen Bishop took the sun and blotted it out from the sky on "Save It for a Rainy Day" (1976), while "On and On" (1978) was just as unremitting in its examination of life's futility. Andrew Gold borrowed the title for "Lonely Boy" (1977) from an old Paul Anka teen hit, but Andrew's version of loneliness was born of a hopelessness that Anka never approached. "Sad Eyes," which hit number one for Robert John in 1979, upped the ante even further: "It's over," Bob announced, a distinct echo of John Lennon's "God" in his carefully chosen words, "turn the other way." When the pain becomes too much, all that's left is denial, retreat, and obliteration. Enter Rupert Holmes, whose "Escape (the Pina Colada Song)" became the last number-one single of the 1970s. As Rome burned and pop music braced itself for the fractious decade ahead, all Rupert could think to do was drink himself into a tropical punch stupor and pass out on the shuffleboard court.

As for the rest of Ronco's foot soldiers, they were all special in their own way. The Starland Vocal Band's "Afternoon Delight" (1976) and Mary MacGregor's "Torn Between Two Lovers" (1977) were as recklessly libidinous as anything from the K-Tel vaults, Mac Davis included. The video for "Two Lovers," where Mary scrawls "Explore

Polygamy" on the tummies of both her boyfriends, was particularly erotic. Debby Boone's K-Tel bloodlines were as strong as Gerry Rafferty's — her father was Daniel Boone of "Beautiful Sunday" fame — and in 1977 she shocked everyone when "You Light Up My Life" became the biggest single of the decade, spending ten weeks at number one. The song was lifted from a Didi Conn film of the same name, and if you listen closely Grandmaster Melle Mel can be heard chanting, "Didi Conn, Didi Conn, let me rock you Didi Conn" in the background. "Don't Give Up On Us" hit number one in 1977 for David Soul, the non-Polish half of *Starsky & Hutch*, making him the only TV detective besides Shaun Cassidy to chart in the seventies, although maybe Rhythm Heritage's "Theme from S.W.A.T."(1975) and "Baretta's Theme" (1976) should also count. The hardcore jazz community pushed Chuck Mangione's "Feels So Good" onto the pop charts in 1978, an incandescent flugel horn workout from a man universally beloved for his floppy hats, beatnik cool, and robust sense of humor.

The urban sophistication of "Feels So Good" could also be heard in Boz Scaggs' "Lowdown" (1976), Starbuck's "Moonlight Feels Right" (1976), and Gino Vanelli's "I Just Wanna Stop" (1978), three records that cried out for a magnum of champagne, a heart-shaped jacuzzi, and a weekend pass for two to Plato's Retreat, New York's infamous late-seventies sex club.[1] Boz and 'Buck operated at the intersection between pop, disco, and SCTV's Rockin' Mel Slurp, an amorphous region that also produced Nick Gilder's "Hot Child in the City," Player's "Baby Come Back," and Exile's "Kiss You All Over," all of which reached number one in 1978. The latter was an especially fascinating mongrel: smouldering quasi-disco produced by the glam-bubblegum team of Chapman/Chinn and performed by a popular country group for the Toto/Supertramp/Earth, Wind & Fire demographic. Ballad honors for the Ronco era went to Walter Egan for "Magnet and Steel" (1978), borderline doo-wop that was really and truly the first lite-metal record ever. And to finish up in grand style was a record that got to the very core of Ronco's ineffable kingdom, Alan O'Day's "Undercover Angel": didn't matter if it was Farrah, Jaclyn, or

---

[1] Gino, of course, had to give back all his awards and gold records when it was revealed he'd one day be confused with Milli Vanilli.

Kate who crawled under there with Al, those little synthesizer blips in the bridge were something to cheer about.

Just as K-Tel was brought to its knees by Ronco, Ronco itself was eventually overtaken by Polytel, which in turn gave way to the half-hour infomercials that command the TV-album market today. Thankfully, there are still vintage thirty-second spots being produced for Kathi Lee Gifford, the Statler Brothers, Victor Borge, Roger Whittaker, and many other artists able to combine a strong sense of pop music history with effective telemarketing skills. K-Tel and Ronco have guided us all the way through the Top Forty war zone of the 1970s, everyone from Norman Greenbaum to C.W. McCall to Robert John, a secret line of succession too often neglected by rock historians obsessed with questions like, "Who's better, the Strawbs or the Mother Love Bones?" — questions that can only to serve to divide us instead of bringing us together. But our journey's over now; it's time to turn the other way.

Chapter 24

THE SECRET LIFE OF WALTER MURPHY

"We aren't the kind of group that's rehearsed in garages or basements — like the Partridge Family — for four or five or six years until you finally get a break."
— Randy of the Village People, 1979.

THE 1970s will always be remembered, first and foremost, for disco. More than any other seventies pop genre, disco was a way of life, one that influenced fashion (thongs, silk shirts, dog whistles), leisure activity (dancing, roller skating, burning records), and television programming (*Dance Fever, Disco Magic ,The Bionic Woman*). Disco's greatest impact, however, was as the pop music of its day. Indeed, one of the most remarkable stories of the decade was just how many non-disco people made disco records — the Rolling Stones, David Bowie, Rod Stewart, Queen, ABBA, and Kiss all climbed aboard, many of them with the biggest hits of their careers. Lots of other big names released less successful crossover attempts (the Beach Boys, the Kinks, James Brown, Dolly Parton, Cher, B.B. King, Donny Osmond's controversial *Disco Train*), while curmudgeons like Lou Reed, Bob Seger, Frank Zappa, and April Wine ("Disco music's just a social disease/If it don't rock me then it ain't gonna please me") released anti-disco diatribes. Guy Lafleur and Telly Savalas made disco records, Bruce Jenner starred in a disco art-film (*Can't Stop the Music*), and Andy Warhol, Lauren Hutton, Pierre Elliot Trudeau, and Gene-Gene-the-Dancing-Machine did the Bump. Little Richard even popped up one day to claim he invented disco, always a sure sign that things were getting completely out of hand.

Right from its inception as an underground subculture in gay and black nightclubs in the early seventies, disco was literally a plastic revolution. Its medium was records, in particular those with a steady, often machine-driven backbeat set somewhere between 120 and 3,000 beats per minute, and featuring more strings per millisecond than a Moody Blues record. Its messenger was the club disc jockey, who blended the most unlikely records together — Isaac Hayes' *Hot Buttered Soul* on turntable 1, *Tomita's Greatest Hits* on turntable 2, *Lola Falana at the Fillmore* on turntable 3 — to create extravagant symphonies for post-adolescents. Its message was clear and direct: Dance! Dance! Dance! aka the 'Yowsah, Yowsah, Yowsah' rule.

All sorts of proto-disco records snuck onto the radio in 1973 (the O'Jays' "Love Train," Sylvia's "Pillow Talk," Eddie Kendricks' "Keep On Truckin'," Manu Dibango's "Soul Makossa," Gilbert O'Sullivan's "Get Down"), and a year later disco officially began its assault on the charts and on the sensibilities of people still recovering from post-Hokey-Pokey trauma left over from grade school. The first bonafide disco smash was Love Unlimited Orchestra's "Love's Theme," an elaborately orchestrated instrumental track by Barry White's backup band that hit number one early in 1974. Barry himself was one of disco's pioneers, charting regularly with growly paeans to pleasure that have never been matched for romantic excess, sweeping string sections, and thoughtful employment of parallel adjectives. "I'm Gonna Love You Just a Little More Baby," "Never, Never Gonna Give You Up" (both 1973), and "Can't Get Enough of Your Love, Babe" (1974) were just three of Barry's legendary moanfests, and if you keep reshuffling the words you'll come up with eight more of his titles. Whether professing true love or simply looking to swim a few laps in the waterbed, the Bear was unfailingly over the top; or, as Barry might have phrased it, very, very, very, truly, truly, *truly* over the top.

Disco was given an even bigger boost in the summer of 1974 when two dance hits went number one back-to-back. First up was the

Hues Corporation's "Rock the Boat," which perfectly bridged the gap between *The Poseidon Adventure* (1972) and Gordon Lightfoot's "The Wreck of the Edmund Fitzgerald" (1976), causing half the people who heard it to shout 'Ahoy!' while the other half went out and purchased lifejackets. Hue and crew were thrown overboard a week later by George McCrae's "Rock Your Baby," a sexy, sprightly, scary song that spawned an almost identical answer record from George's wife, Gwen, a year later ("Rockin' Chair"). Much has been made of the fact that these early disco records contained the word 'rock' in their titles, but Disco Tex & the Sex-O-Lettes' "Get Dancin'" came along late in 1974 to change forever the vocabulary of disco music (Gary's Gang's "Keep on Dancin'," Claudja Barry's "Dancin' Fever," Nigel Olsson's "Dancin' Shoes," the Guess Who's "Dancin' Fool"), giving it an identity of its own. "Get Dancin'" worked on the listener through sheer intimidation: when the towering, sinister, near-maniacal ex-hairdresser Monti Rock III (Disco Tex) told you to get dancin', you didn't ask any questions, you just danced.

"Rock Your Baby" and "Rockin' Chair" were both written and produced by Harry Wayne Casey and Richard Finch, a couple of Miami session players behind KC and the Sunshine Band, an early disco hit machine. On a string of irrepressible singles — most notably "Get Down Tonight," "That's the Way (I Like It)" (both 1975), and "Keep It Comin' Love" (1977) — KC *oohed* and *aahed* divinely, eased our troubled minds, and proved every bit as inspirational as Casey Stengel and Casey Kasem before him. Amidst a disco scene that would increasingly rely upon studio electronics, the relatively earthy Sunshine Band was what you might call 'old school.' So too were the Trammps, a mammoth congregation of trashy trombonists and zany xylophonists who came along shortly thereafter with "The Night the Lights Went Out" (1977), where singer Jimmy Ellis made the best of a traumatic power failure by taking Vicki Lawrence[1] dancing in the dark. The Trammps' biggest hit was "Disco Inferno" (1977), truly one of the decade's most incendiary pop fantasies (Brian Eno's "Baby's on Fire" and Andy Kim's "Fire, Baby I'm on Fire",1974, the Marshall Tucker Band's "Fire on the Mountain", 1975, etc.).

[1.] Still vacationing in New York City while Georgia hydro officials worked to rectify the situation back home.

Barry, KC, Tex, and the Philly International sound all helped set the mirrorball a-spinnin', and by late 1977, with *Saturday Night Fever* bringing disco into neighborhood theatres, the music was suddenly everywhere: roller rinks, drag strips, school cafeterias, fruit and vegetable markets, courtrooms, bowling alleys, public libraries, art galleries, there wasn't an inch of terrain where one wasn't confronted by the pulsating rhythms of disco music. Radio stations across America went all-disco, record companies hired disco consultants, and the United Nations discussed plans to form a worldwide Disco Alliance. Disco was biggest on dance floors, of course, and New York's Studio 54 replaced Mount Rushmore, the Graceland estate, and the game room at the Kennedy compound as the country's prime tourist attraction. The assemblage of characters who frequented Studio 54 was diverse and bizarre — movie stars, foreign dignitaries, Olympic gold-medalists, Dallas Cowboy cheerleaders — and you never knew who you would spot ("Look, it's...it's...Leo Sayer!"). Studio 54's carnival atmosphere was nothing, however, compared to the disco talents, geniuses, and opportunists who raced up the pop charts and, in most cases, plummeted with even greater speed.

The most animated disco cartoons were the Village People, who, unlike Roger Ramjet and Yosemite Sam, espoused a gay sensibility, even if it was coyly left open to question whether the group was really gay or whether they were just very happy. Conceived by French producer Jacques Morali, the People were a melting pot of various male American personas: a cop, a Native Indian, a guy who looked like Gene Autry, a couple of sailors, and a construction worker who doubled as bouncer to "keep things under control." "Macho Man" (1978), their first hit, was an attack on sensitive seventies men ranging from James Taylor to Richard Thomas to Ted Nugent; "Y.M.C.A." (1979) celebrated pick-up basketball, Roman-Greco wrestling, and male bonding; and "In the Navy" (1979) helped to clear up the mystery of their sexuality when it became known that Jimmy Carter was working behind the scenes to lift the ban on gays in the Village People.

Disco novelties came and went with alarming regularity in the second half of the seventies, some out of nowhere, others part of booming subgenres (Big Band Disco, Surf Disco, Singer-Songwriter

Disco, etc.) that showcased disco's penchant for wrapping a 4/4 beat around virtually anything. The most popular spin-off was Classical Disco, thanks to the likes of the Salsoul Orchestra ("Firebird Suite," 1977), Cerrone ("Love in 'C' Minor — Pt. 1," 1977), Walter Murphy, and Meco. Murphy hit number one with "A Fifth of Beethoven" (1976), a highbrow disco concerto that was quickly answered by Herbie Mann's "Roll Over Walter (and Tell Dan Hartman the News)." Meco took "'Star Wars Theme/Cantina Band" (1977) to the top of the charts, but he eventually gave up Classical Disco and turned to plundering the works of his idol, Lou Reed, on *The Velvet Underground and Meco* (1978).

Many other disco artists recalled (and in some instances overlapped with) their counterparts in the K-Tel/Ronco universe, jumping on pop culture fads or icons for aesthetic inspiration. Surprisingly, there was only one specific dance craze during the period, Van McCoy's "The Hustle" (1975). It was a record that shocked the music world: the down-to-the-ground flute, the wake-the-dead violins, the surging cries of "DO THE HUSTLE!" — Van made it all seem secondary, and he also made the Ritchie Family sound like little kids. HRS was a source of countless Boogie Disco hybrids, classics like Claudja Barry's "Boogie Oogie Dancin' Shoes" (1977), A Taste of Honey's "Boogie Oogie Oogie" (1978), and Heatwave's "Boogie Nights" (1978). Rose Royce's soundtrack hit "Car Wash" (1977) was equally blue collar, reminiscent of Jim Croce's "Workin' at the Car Wash Blues" (1974), and its opening handclaps triggered instant memories of the film's prestigious supporting cast (Garrett Morris, Franklin Ajaye, Irwin Corey). Rick Dees' "Disco Duck" (1976) was second only to Ernie's "Rubber Duckie" (1970) as the best Duck Rock song of the decade, with Ernie getting the nod for his cool pre-Travis Bickle mohawk cut. Dees went on to radically redefine the medium of television in the early eighties as host of *Solid Gold,* but he was eventually yanked off the air when he incited viewers to open their windows and shout, "I'm goofy as heck, and I quite like it that way!"

Because disco was fair game for anyone regardless of race, creed, or religion, it's not surprising that people from all over the world hup-two-three-four'd along. Disco factories turned up in France (Alec R. Costandinos' "The Hunchback of Notre Dame," 1978), Canada

147

(Gino Soccio's "Dancer," 1979), Japan (Pink Lady's "Kiss in the Dark," 1977), Spain (Santa Esmeralda's "Don't Let Me Be Misunderstood," 1977), a small patch of land on the tip of New Zealand (Musique's "In the Bush," 1978), and 'parts unknown' (Bimbo Jet's "El Bimbo," 1975). The most prolific world centre was Munich, Germany, where Boney M bruised the egos of rock, reggae, and polka purists by rummaging around for sacred standards (the Melodians' "Rivers of Babylon," Neil Young's "Heart of Gold," Roger Miller's "King of the Road") and taking them to Club Med for a week of fun and games and pina coladas. The group was the brainchild of Frank Farian, who would later write, produce, sing, and perform on — but otherwise have nothing to do with — Milli Vanilli's best-selling *Thoroughly Modern Milli* LP. Although it never charted in North America, the Boneys are primarily remembered for "Rasputin" (1978), a Farian original about "Russia's greatest love machine" that so angered Leonid Brezhnev, he promptly declared Russia a disco-free zone. An even more novel approach to German hedonism was taken by Kraftwerk, four collapsible synthesizer stands who became "extremely excitable" about the new dance sound sweeping the world (it was "Kung Fu Fighting" that turned them around) and responded with "Autobahn" (1975), one of the flukiest records ever to grace the U.S. charts. Be forewarned: do not dance to Kraftwerk and operate heavy machinery at the same time. Kraftwerk's spiritual brethren was female trio Silver Convention, who imported a number-one hit that same year with "Fly, Robin, Fly." The song only had eight words ("Fly, Robin, fly/Up, up to the sky"), 2.67 per member, and the LP it came from featured a pair of handcuffs on the cover. This would seem to have indicated an interest in law enforcement among the girls.

There was one disco moment that was even more bewildering than the Village People, Studio 54, "The Hustle," or Kraftwerk — the sudden and sweeping backlash that occurred as the 1970s came to a close. For manifold reasons that no one's quite figured out yet (some cited homophobia or racism, others blamed *Dance Fever*'s Deney Terrio), millions of people started dissing disco. Longtime booster Norman Mailer switched allegiance from Studio 54 to CBGBs; all-disco stations went to an all-Spud Rock format; Boney M took a nightflight to delete bins; "Disco Sucks" T-shirts were advertised in the back pages of *Rolling Stone*; there was an assassination attempt on Rick Dees; and, worst of all, a huge bonfire of disco records at Chicago's Comiskey Park in August 1979, which was not only a terrible waste of precious vinyl but a perfectly silly reason to cancel a baseball game.

Two of the era's key artists, Chic and Michael Jackson, sent disco off with fitting bon voyages. Chic, a super-sleek organization fronted by Nile Rodgers and Bernard Edwards, were the classiest/cheesiest champagne-sipping pop stars this side of Roxy Music. The group's first big hit was "Dance, Dance, Dance (Yowsah, Yowsah, Yowsah)" (1977), and in 1979 they went to number one twice with "Le Freak" and "Good Times," both covertly chilling antidotes to sunny, end-of-the-disco-era anthems from McFadden & Whitehead ("Ain't No Stoppin' Us Now," 1979), Patrick Hernandez ("Born To Be Alive," 1979), and John Paul Young ("Love Is in the Air," 1979). Meanwhile, Michael Jackson had his secretary put Tito and Jermaine on hold for a year and released *Off the Wall* (1979), his breakthrough solo LP. True to the spirit of Pink Floyd, *Off the Wall* was a disco concept album: it opened with "Don't Stop 'Til You Get Enough," the second *Star Wars* disco epic of the decade, and after moving through a couple of cunning dance-sex metaphors ("Rock With You," "Get On the Floor") and a tearful breakup ("She's Out of My Life"), ended with a promise to "Burn This Disco Out." Whether on his own or with his brothers, from "I Want You Back" to "Dancing Machine" (1974) to "Shake Your Body Down to the Ground" (1979) to *Off the Wall*, the music of Michael Jackson encompassed the entirety of the 1970s — wait a minute, are we in the right decade?

Strictly speaking, "Good Times" and *Off the Wall* didn't draw the curtains on disco *music* anymore than those spoilsports at Comiskey Park; as anyone who has turned on a radio since 1979 can tell you, disco continued to thrive well into the nineties under a variety of pseudonyms ('electro-pop,' 'new romantic,' 'house,' 'deep house,' 'semi-shallow house,' 'isn't that a lovely house'). It's the disco *moment* that has never been matched for cultural dementia — it seemed the freakier you were, the better you fit in, and we never even bothered to mention the Wilton Place Street Band's "Disco Lucy" (or their ill-advised follow-up, "Disco Fred"). But instead of getting tangled up in minutiae, we'll simply take a cue from Michael Jackson and burn this chapter out.

Chapter 25

GO GIRL CRAZY!

"God had to create disco music so that I could be born and be
successful. I was blessed. I am blessed."
— Donna Summer, 1979.

GREAT, weird, ridiculous, and exotic dance hits came from all
over the place in the late seventies, but mostly they were the domain
of young women, inheritors of the early-sixties girl group sound. What
Gloria Gaynor, Sister Sledge, and dozens more took from Darlene
Love and the Chantels was a playful sensuality, a terrific pop sensibility, and oftentimes a male svengali directing the action. The girls of
disco were, by necessity, more outrageous than their predecessors
(sixties cooing became seventies panting, sequined gowns made way
for see-through bodysuits), so the street-wisened punk that the
Shangri-Las immortalized in "Give Him a Great Big Kiss" became an
upwardly mobile member of the medical establishment (Carol Douglas' "Doctor's Orders," 1974), a nattily dressed heartthrob (Sister
Sledge's "He's the Greatest Dancer," 1979), or an oversexed milkman
(Anita Ward's "Ring My Bell," 1979). The pillow talk of girl disco was
good-bad, though, and not by any means evil.

Spearheading this mini-movement was Donna Summer, the

only disco artist with a career résumé to rival David Bowie for sheer eclecticism, ABBA for worldwide popularity, and Marie Osmond for spiritual roots. Originally from Boston, Donna's career began to take shape in Germany in the early seventies, one of a long line of American teenagers whose lives had been irrevocably altered by a chance encounter with Can's *Ege Bamyasi* (1972). It was there that she hooked up with Giorgio Moroder and Pete Bellotte, two studio producers at work on a revolutionary branch of disco they hoped would appeal to Barry White, Tangerine Dream, and *Deep Throat* fans alike. The team's first success was "Love To Love You Baby" (1975), seventeen minutes of metronomic intensity and dramatic orchestral manoeuvres that had Donna achieving (or faking, or method-acting) orgasm twenty-two times. The song was banned from radio play in some quarters (a shortened version made the Top Ten anyway) when it was judged to be obscene. After spending months studying the mysterious sounds that emanate from Donna's mouth, however, we can safely conclude that they are unintelligible at any speed.

Donna and her producers followed with some less successful rehashes of "Love To Love You Baby," after which they began to expand their horizons on some of the most delectable hits of the disco era: "I Feel Love" (1977) was bubble-disco of the highest order, Kraftwerk jumping for joy at their discovery of the Ohio Express' "Yummy Yummy Yummy"; on "Last Dance" (from the movie *Thank God It's Friday*) and a cover of Richard Harris' "MacArthur Park" (both 1978), Donna veered off into the snazziest Showtune Disco this side of Ethel Merman's discofied remake of "There's No Business Like Show Business" (1979); and "Hot Stuff" (1979) was first-rate disco-metal that out-discoed the Stones' "Hot Stuff," just as the cover of Donna's *Bad Girls* (1979) promised a better time than *Some Girls*.[1]

Donna's last major hit of the seventies was "No More Tears (Enough is Enough)" (1979), a much-ballyhooed collaboration with Barbara Streisand that also happened to be the last number-one song of the disco era. It wasn't Donna's last dance, however — she continued to chart records through the eighties, though she alienated

---

[1] As far as Calender Rock went, Donna was cleaning up — the Fall were just getting started, Spring was long gone, Edgar Winter was in limbo, and the Four Seasons were still adjusting to the departure of Frankie Valli.

much of her loyal fan base when she began flirting with Moral Majorityism as the decade wound down. Regardless, Donna was truly one of the seventies' great wanderers, and we remain lost forever without her.

The rest of the girl disco universe included all types: soul-stirring chanteuses and mechanical studio robots, performance artists and *Gong Show* contestants, one-hit wonders and three-hit colossuses. The only performers who posed any sort of a challenge to Donna were Gloria Gaynor and Sylvester. Gloria charted one of the genre's earliest hits, 1974's transcendent "Never Can Say Goodbye," and in 1979 she went to number one with "I Will Survive," a rallying cry many years later for the Grateful Dead in their Acid House/Top Forty phase. Sylvester put aside an illustrious gospel career — 1973's "Down on Your Knees" was a Sunday school favorite — to pursue hypnotic synthesizer rhythms on "Dance (Disco Heat)" (1978) and "I (Who Have Nothing)" (1979). On "You Make Me Feel (Mighty Real)" (1979), his masterpiece, Syl's repeated cries of "I feel real, I feel real, I feel real" did battle with a wall of Oberheim DS-2 sequencers in a one-of-a-kind ontological cage-match.

Turning to disco's second echelon of girls, Shirley & Company (a descendent of fifties R&B duo Shirley and Lee) made perhaps the unlikeliest comeback of the seventies with "Shame, Shame, Shame" (1975); on the album's cover, Shirley tsk-tsk'ed Richard Nixon for crimes ranging from Watergate to big jowls to the silly polka-dotted tie he was wearing. Vicki Sue Robinson and Amii Stewart had R&B roots too — Vicki paying homage to her elders on 1976's "Turn the Beat Around" ("Love to hear Con-Funk-Shun!"), Amii's frantic cover of Eddie Floyd's "Knock on Wood" (1979) — which they twisted inside out in a typical display of disco irreverence. Amii even dressed up as a pineapple, landing her some commercial spots as the Hawaiian Punch Guy's love interest.

While vocalists like Maxine Nightingale ("Right Back Where We Started From," 1976), Thelma Houston ("Don't Leave Me This Way," 1977), and the Emotions ("Best of My Love," 1977) alluded to primal human urges without once making explicit reference to them, some of the genre's most erotic hits were as up front as "Love To Love You Baby." Nineteen seventy-six was a particularly naughty year, led by

Andrea True Connection's "More, More, More," a soft-core epic sung by a real-life actress in the field (*True's Confessions, The Love Connection , My Dinner With Andrea*). Montreal's Patsy Gallant shot and scored big in Canada with "From New York to L.A.," but her frank depiction of disco life ("The city life, the flashing lights/Busy streets and fancy cars/Using drugs in all the clubs/Everyone's a shining star") and peek-a-boo album covers discouraged American airplay. One person to take notice was Diana Ross, whose finest post-Supremes moment, "Love Hangover," chronicled the morning-after effects of galavanting from St. John's to Victoria with Patsy.

The female disco singers of the late seventies — and we left out a couple hundred, including Cheryl Lynn, Alicia Bridges, Tina Charles, Hot, Evelyn 'Champagne' King, and Jobriath — provided more fun and good cheer than virtually anything else from the era. Unlike Donna, most of them disappeared from public view almost instantly. Their finest work has been preserved on any number of high-quality Ronco compilations, though, where they're still doing a lonely and forgotten dance alongside Fotomaker and Nick Gilder.

Chapter 26

Tie Me Kangaroo Down, Sport

"Making *Sgt. Pepper* was an exciting, educational tease. Now I know
how a major film works, and I know I want more of it."
— Maurice Gibb, 1979.

ALTHOUGH disco was a major force on pop radio as early as 1975,
the genre initially lacked a group or figure that middle America could
identify with, a Great White Hope — an Elvis, a Dylan, a Bo Donaldson
— to take it into shopping malls, grab the headlines of *People*
magazine, and make disco accessible to the vast record-buying public
alienated by Silver Convention's complicated Euro-African rhythms.
There were many worthy candidates for the role — KC and Rick Dees
especially — but the search ended with the release of *Saturday Night
Fever* in 1977. The Bee Gees, an Australian brother act who provided
most of the music for the blockbuster film, were the most unlikely
disco superstars of all: not only were they relative old-timers, but they
danced about as well as the Beach Boys surfed. That they did measure
up, and did so on such a resounding worldwide scale, was the sort of
thing which could only make sense in the seventies.

Barry, Robin, and Maurice Gibb got their start in the mid-sixties,
when time and time again they took their three-square vocal attack
to the top of Australian charts. Their masterpiece during this formative

period was 1966's "Spicks and Specks," a Dylan-styled dream narrative: "Spicks and specks/Specks and spicks/Death and cornflakes/Just don't mix." The group moved to England in 1967, teaming up with producer/manager Robert Stigwood for a long string of international pop hits. Among the highlights were "(The Lights Went Out In) Massachusetts" (1967), "Words" (1968), and "I Started a Joke" (1968), the latter of which earned the group the respect of stand-up comedians the world over, and later inspired the Minutemen to wonder *What Makes a Man Start Jokes?* The Bee Gees released their only pre-disco number-one single in 1971, "How Can You Mend a Broken Heart?," but after a couple more hits they suddenly disappeared from public view. As the 'Gees themselves tell the story, the problems were internal—drug abuse, contractual disputes, Maurice's inability to complete a long-rumored rock opera based on "Spicks and Specks"—but it was just as true that the group's sensitive brand of pop was starting to sound quaint next to the gargantuan clamor of Led Zeppelin and the technocratic sophistication of Deodato. The low point came in 1974 when their record label refused to release a finished LP entitled *A Kick in the Head Is Worth Eight in the Pants* . No one's ever heard these long lost songs, but it's a title that doesn't deserve to go unused.

Australians have always been known for their ability to bounce back, though, so later that year Stigwood introduced the Bee Gees to Arif Mardin, an R&B producer of the highest calibre (Aretha Franklin, Average White Band, Richard Harris). With Mardin on hand, the Bee Gees adopted a looser, less Caucasian feel, not so much an effort to go disco (especially since no one was yet 100% sure where you were supposed to go) as to simply sound more contemporary. The strategy paid off on *Main Course* (1975), which featured the Top Forty dance hits "Nights on Broadway" and "Jive Talkin'," the group's first number-one single in four years and the most electrifying stuttering this side of "My Generation" and Porky Pig. They repeated the trick the following year with the heavily discofied "You Should Be Dancing," an intense religious awakening for older fans who were still camped out in Massachusetts waiting for the lights to come on.

As impressive as the Bee Gees' newfound success was, it in no way prepared the world for what followed: *Saturday Night Fever*, a disco movie starring John Travolta as the appealingly dunce-like Tony Manero, with a soundtrack that dominated the airwaves for the next twelve months like nothing else in the seventies. Many of *Saturday Night Fever*'s most indelible images were those featuring the Gibbs trilling away in the background — Travolta combing his hair to "Night Fever" and stuffing his face with pizza to "Staying Alive," the Truffaut-like freeze frame of "How Deep Is Your Love" — and the Bee Gees became the Crazy-Glue that held this brave new vision of America together. It was a vision best summed up in Tony's response to his boss's advice that he save his money and plan for the future: "*Tonight* is the future," Tony fired back, "and I *am* planning for it." For reasons best explained by sociologists, America embraced this version of no-future while rejecting Johnny Rotten's.

Saturday Night Fever's soundtrack also included some older Bee Gees numbers, instrumentals by David Shire and Walt Murphy, Travolta's famous "Are you talking to me?" monologue from the film, an interview with Stigwood, Monti Rock III reciting "Almost Cut Tony's Hair," and hits by Yvonne Elliman ("If I Can't Have You") and Tavares ("More Than a Woman"). By early 1978, it seemed as if the Bee Gees and Stigwood's RSO record label had a stranglehold on American singles charts: hits from the movie *Grease* (Frankie Valli's title track, Travolta's and Olivia Newton-John's "You're the One That I Want"), Player's "Baby Come Back," Samantha Sang's "Emotion" (written by Barry and Robin), and even another Gibb, little brother Andy, who made it to number one with "I Just Want To Be Your Everything" (1977), "Love Is Thicker Than Water" (1978), and "Shadow Dancing" (1978). Besides writing and producing the bulk of Andy's material, the Bee Gees also chipped in with background vocals on many of Andy's hits. When the entire Gibb posse got together for "Shadow Dancing," the results were volcanic: "Ready Maurice?...Barry?...Robin?...Well all right Gibbs — LET'S GO!"

In the fall of 1978, the Bee Gees lent their clout to a cinematic adaptation of *Sgt. Pepper's Lonely Hearts Club Band* ,[1] where they starred alongside Peter Frampton (Billy Shears), George Burns (Mr. Kite), Rita Coolidge (the meter maid), and Maurice White (the space

---

[1] After reluctantly turning down offers to bring Floyd's *Atom Heart Mother*, Edgar Froese's *Aqua*, and Return to Forever's *The Leprechaun* to the big screen.

between them all). The film proved to be the missing link between *Cleopatra* and *Ishtar* in the annals of movie bellyflopdom, taking down Frampton, Aerosmith, and Billy Preston with it, but initially the Bee Gees were able to withstand the shock. Their follow-up to *Saturday Night Fever*, 1979's *Spirits Having Flown*, generated another three number-one hits ("Too Much Heaven," "Tragedy," and "Love You Inside Out"), bringing their total for the decade to an unsurpassed nine. ABC television even launched a nightly Bee Gees watch called *Night Fever Line: America Held Hostage*.

But the disco backlash caught up to the Gibbs soon enough. If anything, they came up for the greatest beating of all — it was so severe, they still only pop out from the ground every five years or so, tentatively checking for flying objects much as a groundhog checks for its shadow. Too bad, because seventies pop didn't get much better than "Jive Talkin'," "You Should Be Dancing," or "Night Fever," and the Bee Gees deserve credit for bringing disco to millions of listeners who might otherwise have missed all the fun. Besides, it's not polite to make fun of Australians.

Chapter 27

WAKE ME UP BEFORE YOU POGO

" I don't understand why people think it's so difficult to learn to play guitar. I found it incredibly easy. You just pick a chord, go twang, and you've got music."
— Sid Vicious, 1976.

For all the considerable squawking it engendered, disco was hardly the only musical development in the mid-to-late seventies to confound and disgust the comatose rock audience. The Bee Gees, Donna, KC, and the rest of the Village Metronomes was one kind of ambush; a second and equally disorienting attack was launched right around the time disco started to take off, and this one was so apocalyptic that it even roused the Eagles' Don Henley from an afternoon nap long enough for him to mumble, "Punk? Why, Kool & the Gang invented punk years ago — or maybe that was James Brown — I'm sorry, could you repeat the question?" Indeed, trying to trace the genesis of punk is as contentious and murky a task as similar attempts with heavy metal, especially as whole books have been written trying to prove they're the same thing. There's no time for that here; besides, every sensible person knows that punk began in the days of the Flintstones, when disaffected citizens adopted crude surnames like 'Rubble,' 'Slate,' and 'Granite' as a gesture of utter contempt for societal norms. We'll instead pick up the story at an acknowledged turning point, New York City in 1975, where a decrepit Lower East Side bar named CBGBs began featuring scrawny looking rock bands instead of its usual country and western fare. CBGBs' change in policy had drastic and far-reaching repercussions: country music, for starters, immediately relocated to Nashville, Tennessee, where in 1983 the Grand Ole Opry would be built.

The biggest initial splash out of CBGBs was made by Patti Smith, a junior-cub scenemaker and occasional *Creem* contributor who'd been kicking around since the early seventies. Like Jim Morrison and Chubby Checker before her, Smith's two greatest passions in life were rock and roll and obscure French Symbolist poetry, so one day she hired a band and commenced reciting her impenetrable scribblings over a three-chord woolly-bully beat. On Smith's debut album, *Horses* (1975), she bonyed some here, maronyed a little there, put her hand inside her boyfriend's cranium, and a strange new kind of insurrection-ary music was born.

Tom Verlaine and Richard Hell were also familiar faces around CBGBs, and together they founded the band Television, who would eventually release a famous LP called *Marquee Moon* (1977). With their emphasis on long songs and slow tempos and complicated guitar solos, Television really didn't have much to do with punk as performed by such latter-day stars as the Plasmatics, Sigue Sigue Sputnik, and Doctor & the Medics. Richard, who had departed Television by the time *Marquee Moon* appeared, also fronted the Voidoids on their highly influential "Blank Generation" (1976). This was more than just hell, wary observers noted at the time, this was Richard Hell.

If punk had stopped there, listening to it today would feel a lot like homework. But there was another CBGBs band, the Ramones, that took a very different route to the ignominious realm of public ridicule. Comprised of four brothers from the tiny country of Ramonia, the Ramones wrote songs that mirrored their environment and tried to make sense of the human experience: "I don't wanna walk around with you/So why you wanna walk around with me?" they wondered, a dilemma that originated with Socrates (whose walking partners were crucial to the whole Socratic method), except the Ramones figured they didn't need any other lyrics because words get in the way. It made for a clean break from the verbal overload of seventies pop, as did the extra-accelerated tempo of their music — same three chords as Patti and the Stooges and the ninth section of the second movement of King Crimson's "Dance of the Phosphorescent Willow Trees #11," but rammed out so breathlessly that each song clocked in around the two-minute mark. The Ramones 'honed their craft' for a couple years around CBGBs, then released four LPs that ached nostalgically for rock and roll before it became rock: *Ramones* (1976), *Leave Home* and *Rocket to Russia* (1977), and *Road to Ruin* (1978). Anyone who heard the Ramones either loved or hated them passionately. People of both viewpoints expressed concern that Joey Ramone looked undernourished and a little otherworldly.

There has always been some debate over how much the Ramones influenced parallel events unfolding in England at the time: some say a lot, some say not at all, many lead perfectly normal lives without having any opinion whatsoever. For the sake of simplicity, though, let's say that everything so far has been background din and that punk really began with the Sex Pistols, who popped up on King's Road one day and proceeded to turn the entire decade upside down. The Pistols' focal point was their singer, Johnny Rotten (real name Murray Rotten), an extremely cantankerous street urchin who heaped scorn on his country, his queen, his audience, his record label, his contemporaries, sex, food, the past, the future, anything and everything he held court on. He was so mean, he didn't even spare a kind word for Georgette from *The Mary Tyler Moore Show*. Rounding out the band were Sid Vicious, a classically trained flautist and accidental inventor of the pogo dance;[1] Steve Jones, a no-goodnik so big and tough he sometimes wore women's hairnets just because he knew no one would make fun of him; and Paul Cook, who was clearly embarrassed to be Steve's good friend. An earlier member, Glen Matlock, was booted out upon admitting he was a major Edison Lighthouse fan.

From late 1975, when they were assembled by legendary British

---

[1] "I dunno," Sid later explained, "I suddenly felt this surge of ecstatic benevolence pass through me , an inner knowledge that John had it all wrong, and I just had to jump around a bit."

talent scout Malcolm McLaren, to their final performance as halftime entertainment at the 1978 Super Bowl in San Francisco, everything about the Sex Pistols scandalized and terrorized the world of pop music even by its own loutish standards of behavior. In one of the band's earliest misdeeds, Steve and Paul nicked some musical equipment from David Bowie; seems that Steve was so impressed by the white-soul ambience of *Young Americans*, he went right to the source in hopes of duplicating it. In 1976 the Pistols made headlines by spouting rude language on a venerable TV talk show, and by year's end they'd been kicked off two record labels before they even got an album out, a truly ingenious way to earn severance pay. The following summer, Johnny greeted the news of Elvis' death by saying "Good riddance to bad rubbish," perhaps the tenderest eulogy of all for the fallen King.

If the Pistols' words and actions were cause for dismay, their music provoked everything from temporary itching to aneurysms. "Anarchy in the U.K." (1976), their first single, sounded like no rock and roll before or since, not unless you count Mark Lindsay's demented cries of "Cherokee people!" on the Raiders' "Indian Reservation." The Pistols continued to spread good cheer throughout 1977 with "God Save the Queen," "Pretty Vacant," "Holidays in the Sun" (probable inspiration for Robin Leach's *Runaway With the Rich and Famous* TV travelogue), and the album that collected their singles and more, *Never Mind the Bollocks, Here's the Sex Pistols*. But before they had a proper chance to get fat and silly and release a live album, the Pistols returned their instruments to Mr. Bowie and dispersed amidst much mutual acrimony in early 1978. Johnny (re-emerging as Murray) started an arty new dub-fusion band, Steve and Paul opened up a scuba-gear shop in Brazil, and Sid wandered off to New York with his girlfriend for an eternity of undisturbed domestic bliss. Perhaps Queen Elizabeth summed up the Pistols' legacy best: "They were a splendid band, absolutely first-rate. Britain will miss them very much."

The second most famous punk band after the Pistols was the Clash, four regular yobs with thick British accents, big thoughtful hearts, widespread populist appeal, and really corny shirt collars. In marked contrast to the Pistols, who pretty much lived to get under people's skin and start chewing, the Clash sought solutions — to class oppression, to racial tension, to social apathy, to whatever called for sitting themselves down, thinking through the problem, and coming up with a solution. (Jumble Word Puzzles were a particular band favorite.) The Clash, their first LP from 1977, always turns up on greatest-ever lists today, and it even managed to look optimistically toward a future that Johnny Rotten couldn't envision: right in the middle of side one, for no apparent reason, singer Joe Strummer started ranting, "Quiet Riot, I wanna Riot, Quiet Riot, I wanna Riot of my own!" Unfortunately, all Joe got was a Blue Oyster Cult of his own, as BOC producer Sandy Pearlman forced the band into a half-hearted fling with Satanic sex rituals and Druid costumes on Give 'Em Enough Rope (1978).

The Clash's mystique continued to grow, however, and by 1979 they were billing themselves as 'the only band that matters.' The slogan caught on, so others jumped in with much less success. The ever suave Roxy Music became 'the only band that brunches,' Earth, Wind & Fire tried 'the only band that levitates,' and eco-nuts Seals and Crofts went with 'the only band that car pools.' As the final few seconds of the seventies ticked away, the Clash hit paydirt with London Calling, an amusement-park sampler of monumental proportions.

With the Pistols and the Clash opening up the floodgates, the disco explosion soon had its evil twin sister in the punk explosion of 1977-78. New punk bands appeared at a rate of twelve or fourteen before lunch every day, in Canada, in Australia, in politically volatile danger zones like Akron, Ohio, but most of all in Britain, which remained the center of punk activity. A bunch of Cro-Magnons named the Damned got a record out even before the Pistols, the totally inane, totally fabulous "New Rose" (1976), looking at the time as if they'd only last till they got their first good look at each other and fled pronto. But not only did they stick around for a whole album, 1977's Damned Damned Damned, they released more and more of them because nobody once thought to tell them not to.

Billy Idol also slithered out of the British punk scene, getting his start as lead haircut for Generation X. At a time when Punk Rule #1 in England was a total disdain for all music not punk, Generation X's "Ready Steady Go" (1978) was a touching declaration of Billy's love for the Beatles, Bob Dylan, Rare Earth, and other big-beat greats. The Jam was likewise on a Sha Na Na trip, and on LPs like *In the City* (1977) and *All Mod Cons* (1978) they obsessed on the days when British mods and rockers went down to the beach and beat each other senseless because they didn't know how to play volleyball and had to fill their weekends somehow. Turning to the more exotic, Siouxsie & the Banshees hitched a ride on the Orient Express for the majestic "Hong Kong Garden" (1978), the only punk single that left you hungry an hour later. And then there was the Stranglers, who in unadulterated buffoonery stood mighty tall in the seventies scheme of things. What you need to know about them: 1) they reminded people of the Doors; 2) they recorded two incredible songs, "(Get a) Grip (on Yourself)" (1977) and "Tank" (1978); 3) they didn't *really* drive their very own tank, that was General McArthur; 4) they were rock pigs supreme; 5) they can't be killed.

Moving up three thousand notches on the evolutionary scale, X-Ray Spex, the Adverts, Wire, and the Buzzcocks were four of the best British punk bands around. X-Ray Spex was unusual in that they had a saxophone player; outside of Southside Johnny & the Asbury Jukes, who sometimes sat in with the Spex, they were the only punk band with their own brass section. Throw in the unique warble of Poly Styrene, and X-Ray's *Germfree Adolescents* (1978) was one of the decade's most exciting LPs — it even had a song about crazed teenagers stalking the aisles of Woolworth's, a sure sign that the whole social structure was imploding. The Adverts' "Gary Gilmore's Eyes" (1977) not only inspired Kim Carnes' "Bette Davis Eyes," it became one of the first punk singles to make the Top Twenty in Britain. To commemorate their momentous achievement, the Adverts got together with the Pistols, the Stranglers, and the Damned, and they all did some handstands in Picadilly Circus. Wire was something of a throwback to Patti Smith and television's Dick Cavett in the we've-seen-subtitled-films-and-you-haven't department, but *Pink Flag* (1977) and *Chairs Missing* (1978) had lots — *lots* — of short and snappy songs anyway. The Buzzcocks were one of the first punk groups to emerge from a studio with their jittery *Spiral Scratch* EP (1977), after which Pete Shelley led them through a much beloved series of singles eventually collected on *Singles Going Steady* (1979). One was called

"Orgasm Addict," one was called "Just Lust," one was called "Why Can't I Touch It?"— put 'em together and the obvious answer is, "Because you might end up breaking it in half, Peter."

The number of great punk records to come out of Britain was seemingly endless: the Swell Maps' "Read About Seymour" (1977), the Vibrators' *Pure Mania* (1977), Stiff Little Fingers' "Alternative Ulster" (1978), plus forgotten classics from the Slits, Sham 69, the Lurkers, 999, Eater (who were too young to see *Saturday Night Fever* without parental accompaniment), and many others. As Plastic Bertrand said upon visiting England in 1978, "Ca plane pour moi!" ("I am surrounded by punk bands, nihilism closes in on all sides, madness and despair overtake me, darkness everywhere!")

The world at large wasn't nearly as punk-crazy as Britain, but there was nevertheless lots of noise being made in other quarters, too. In New York, the Dead Boys ("Sonic Reducer," 1977) became a house favorite at CBGBs thanks to the matinee good-looks of singer Stiv Bators and the richly textured guitar technique of Cheetah Chrome. The Germs ("Forming," 1977) and the Avengers ("The Amerikan in Me," 1978) hailed from San Francisco, with the Germs' Darby Crash setting new standards in befuddlement over one's surroundings. Canada's best punk group was Toronto's Viletones, who on songs like "Screamin' Fist" (1977) and "Don't You Lie" (1978) provided a rousing compendium of every punk cliché imaginable. Australia's the Saints sounded like the early Rolling Stones on "(I'm) Stranded" (1977), and they're still remembered for their legendary debut gig at Kylie Minogue's seventh birthday party. And although punk never achieved quite the international reach of disco, Iceland's Polar Freeze left behind some memorable records too.

For a couple years, punk managed to bore its way into every nook and cranny of the pop consciousness. It elicited an indignant, condescending, and slightly nervous response from Mick Jagger, Rod Stewart, Keith Emerson, and most of the solidly entrenched rock stars of the seventies. (An admirable few — Neil Young, Pete Townshend, Stephen Bishop of course — empathized with and understood this new music.) Suddenly, the simplest everyday gestures became charged with controversy, confrontation, and confusion — not to mention consternation, contradiction, and consistently convoluted conjecture.

But by 1978, punk rock in the spirit of the Sex Pistols, the Adverts, the Dead Boys, and the rest was more or less played out. It became an anachronism, an albatross, and it didn't sell many records. That was the biggest problem of all — everyone talked about punk, but there were only 129 punk records sold in total. A few bands discovered a way around this stumbling block, and pretty soon punk had a new sound, a new haircut, and a new name.

Chapter 28

ALL WE ARE SAYING IS GIVE THE POLICE A CHANCE

"I feel very safe in cars. You can lock the doors and they can't get
to you. I don't like people gettin' to me...People will hurt me."
— Gary Numan, 1980.

HAPPILY, the 1970s went out with a flourish of pop activity as
sublime and ridiculous as all that had set the stage beforehand: new
wave, which was about the only safe thing to label oneself in the last
few months of 1979 if you didn't want to be ostracized by the public
at large. New wave got around this dilemma by secretly pilfering bits
and pieces from all the seventies genres that had, by then, been more
or less discredited: synth aerobics from disco, puppy lust anthems
from the teen riot squad, a 'back to basics' stance derived from HRS,
eyeliner and space gear from glam, complicated electronic circuits
from art rock, and an addiction to novelty that recalled K-Tel at its
finest (Hot Butter, Reunion, and the Record Selector were totally new
wave). Mostly, though, new wave was an offspring of punk, and
trying to determine who was punk and who was new wave became
a matter of considerable discomfiture within the rock star community
as the seventies wound down. Paul Weller begged to be called a punk,
the Rezillos and Ian Gomm argued passionately for the sanctity of new

wave, Talking Heads insisted they belonged to neither camp, and Billy Joel simply shrugged and said, "New wave, next wave, it's all part of an evolutionary process that started with Futurism at the turn of the century and remains viable to this day."

Actually, there were two different new waves to usher out the seventies: the first was new wave music performed by Eraserheads, the second was new wave microsurgery performed by Coneheads. Eraserhead wave was primarily the province of starry-eyed pop enthusiasts — located somewhere between the Swinging Blue Jeans and the Banana Splits — who wore matching black-knit or red-vinyl suits with un-matching green shoes and purple socks. Henry Spencer, the handsome young hero of 1978's *Eraserhead*, gave the movement its name; Lenny & Squiggy and NBC newsman Irving R. Levine were also prototypical Eraserheads. Coneheads, on the other hand, banded together behind three basic principles: the conviction that synthesizers were the wave of the future (and even if they weren't there were still lots of fun buttons to push and mysterious wires to diddle around with); an ability to while away hour after hour browsing their local Radio Shack; and their oft-repeated claim that they had nothing whatsoever to do with rock and roll, "not even Gino Vanelli" as Pere Ubu's David Thomas put it. The Coneheads had their own nominal leader in Beldar of *Saturday Night Live*'s Conehead family; Leroy Jetson, Mr. Wizard, and Governor Jerry Brown were also obvious forerunners .

One of the first Eraserhead bands to pop up in America, getting its start alongside the Ramones and Television at CBGBs, was Blondie, a sextet fronted by ex-glitter girl/ex-Playboy bunny Debbie Harry. Blondie's first two albums (1977's *Blondie* and 1978's *Plastic Letters)* were relegated to cult status, but *Parallel Lines* (1978) was a new wave breakthrough. The LP pushed its way into the Top Ten on the strength of two hit singles ("Heart of Glass" and "One Way or Another"), got the group onto *American Bandstand*, and popularized a late seventies sex symbol to rival Linda Ronstadt, Stevie Nicks, and John Travolta: bassist Nigel Harrison, whose madcap mugging on the album's cover just drove women crazy with desire. "Heart of Glass" was the first hugely successful new wave-disco crossover, so not surprisingly it was greeted with all sorts of petulant complaining from devout pogo-stick people who were politically opposed to moving sideways or back-and-forth. The clamor subsided a few months later when John Lydon was spotted at Studio 54 chatting up the Sex-O-Lettes.

The most popular Eraserheads were the Cars, who bore an uncanny resemblance to Queen in many respects (and were therefore often mistaken for Coneheads). Both groups were produced by Roy Thomas Baker, both harmonized like operatic glee clubs, both looked vaguely human, and both evoked 'feelings of uneasiness' among their fans. Nevertheless, *The Cars* (1978) abounded with short, catchy songs (particularly "Just What I Needed" and "My Best Friend's Girl"), and Ric Ocasek's *Battlestar Galactica* haircut endeared the group to millions. Their biggest hit of the seventies, "Let's Go" (1979), further solidified the emerging new wave-disco alliance, as Ric's stirring declaration that "I love the night life, baby!" paid explicit homage to Alicia Bridges.

Making the swiftest rise to fame and notoriety among new wavers was the Knack, an L.A. foursome who stormed North American pop charts in 1979 with "My Sharona" and "Good Girls Don't." Like the Sex Pistols and the Bay City Rollers before them, the Knack elicited strong reactions from all sides: teenagers looked up to them the way previous generations had looked up to Ernie Douglas on *My Three Sons* ("Here's how to look funny," the Knack's very presence implied, "*now go do it* "); parents feared the misogynist slant of their lyrics ("My Sharona is bigger than your Sharona," boasted singer Doug Fieger); and members of the Dwight Twilley fan club called Fieger's bluff when it was learned that he "had never even listened to the first Big Star album." The group suffered a backlash as staggering as disco's when their peers on the L.A. club scene (the Germs, X, Black Flag) started a vicious 'Knuke the Knack' campaign in late 1979. Heroically, Jackson Browne came to the rescue by organizing an all-star 'Kno Knukes, the Knack Are OK People' concert, with all proceeds going directly into a fund that protected the Rubinoos, Pezband, and other Eraserhead favorites against similar harassment.

No one else in the field achieved quite the chart success of Blondie, the Cars, or the Knack, but there was plenty of action happening on the sidelines and over in the U.K., usually in the form of 'power pop,' 'pub rock,' 'power-pub pop-rock,' and other confusing subdivisions of Eraserhead wave. Out of Zion, Illinois, came the Shoes, who released one perfect album (1978's *Black Vinyl Shoes*) and one pretty good one (1979's *Present Tense*). Unfortunately, the group became a frequent target of terrorist attacks after PLO leader Yasir Arafat labelled them militant Zionists and asked that they be "dealt with accordingly." L.A.'s Moon Martin wrote a future hit for Robert Palmer (1978's "Bad Case of Loving You") and recorded a couple LPs of his own, but he's mostly remembered today for his popular *Moon Martin Celebrity New Wave Roasts*, jovial monthly affairs where Wazmo Nariz's cries of "Never got a dinner!" used to bring the house down. We could continue listing names forever — 20/20, the Pop, the Rubinoos, the Diodes, Rachel Sweet, the Cathode Rays, the Twizzlers, Rotate! — but we'd best cross the ocean before new wave Anglophiles start to get panicky.

In Britain, the Eraserhead uprising was usually associated with pub rock, a movement launched in 1968 by the Irish Rovers ("The Unicorn") and popularized in the mid-seventies by Dr. Feelgood, Ducks Deluxe, and Foster Brooks. Pub rock and new wave eventually came together in the person of Graham Parker, who really wasn't new wave at all — *Howlin' Wind* and *Heat Treatment* (both 1976) recalled Van Morrison, Wilson Pickett, and Tower of Power — but because he looked kind of ill-tempered he created an opening for Elvis Costello and Joe Jackson, both of whom *were* new wave, at least until they started setting their sights on *Time-Life* jazz collections of their work.

Legend has it that Declan McManus was so ticked off for being refused entry onto the set of *Dance Fever* as a teenager (the full details can be heard on his 1977 song "No Dancing"), he changed his name to the much more appealing 'Elvis Costello' and decided to try his hand at new wave. Elvis's first three LPs (*My Aim Is True*, 1977; *This Year's Model*, 1978; *Armed Forces*, 1979) went a long way toward propelling him to King Eraserhead (at least until the ascension of Lyle Lovett), but his biggest headlines were made in 1979 when he triggered a barroom brawl by calling Thor a "big ignorant Viking." Joe Jackson's debut LP, *Look Sharp!* (1979), featured an American hit in "Is She Really Going Out With Him?," an expression of Joe's total disbelief upon learning that Elvis was dating Bebe Buell. Jackson created some controversy of his own when he conspired to fix the 1979 World

Series, causing him to be barred from ever again singing the national anthem at major sporting events.

Although there were other notable records to come out of the pubs — Nick Lowe's "So It Goes" (1976), Ian Dury's "Sex & Drugs & Rock & Roll" (1977), the Records' "Starry Eyes" (1979), and of course the Rovers' "Wasn't That a Party" (1980), which pretty much killed off pub rock altogether — British Eraserheads veered off in any number of directions. The Police did for reggae what Shaun Cassidy did for surf music — got it all wrong and made it stupid-fun — and they also gave us one of rock music's great intellects in Sting Sumner ('Gordon'), one of an illustrious line of school-teachers-turned-pop-stars (Gene Simmons, Gregory Abbott, Professor Longhair). "Roxanne" (1978) was the Police's most popular song of the seventies, but "Message in a Bottle" from the following year was their most prophetic — right around the same time, John Bonham and Bon Scott started finding messages in bottles too. The Pretenders' self-titled 1979 debut had an excellent Kinks cover ("Stop Your Sobbing"), a well placed obscenity on "Precious," a big hit in "Brass in Pocket (I'm Special)," and it tied the Allman Brothers' *Live at the Fillmore East, New York Dolls,* and many Lynyrd Skynyrd albums for the unenviable title of Seventies-LP-with-the-Most-Future-Dead- People (Pete Farndon and James Honeyman Scott).

Ireland's Boomtown Rats veered perilously close to Bruce Springsteen and Meat Loaf at times, but "I Don't Like Mondays" (1979) served as inspiration for both Pearl Jam's "Jeremy" and Dolly Parton's "9 to 5." Another Irish band, the Undertones (not to be confused with the Viletones, the Cretones, the Fleshtones, the Harptones, Tony! Toni! Toné!, Tones on Tail, or Klaus Nomi) released a superb self-titled album in 1979 where they jumped around, made funny faces, and sounded a lot like the Ramones. The Monks were so new wave they were the only U.K. band in history with fake British accents; on "Drugs in My Pocket" (1979), they never even had a chance to complete the song's key lyric — "and I don't know what to do with them"— before the Eagles, Fleetwood Mac, and the Doobie Brothers were lined up at their door looking for leftovers.

Time now to switch the focus to new wave Coneheads. The most widely acclaimed among them was Talking Heads, CBGBs barflys who were brought together by their mutual love of Jean-Luc Godard, KC & the Sunshine Band, ironing boards, neo-expressionism, nail clippers, and filing cabinets. The group pursued a buoyant, arty path on their three albums in the seventies, all of which were dominated by rubber-necked, human whoopie cushion David Byrne, the Charlie Callas of rock and roll. *Talking Heads '77* gained notice for "Psycho Killer," the tale of a serial murderer who did in his victims with a torturous Otis Redding impression; *More Songs About Buildings and Food* (1978) had Eno on board, only one song about buildings and food ("The Big Country"), and a detailed explanation of the color scheme used on its back cover photo that made for first-rate entertainment; *Fear of Music* (1979) was highlighted by "Life During Wartime," the culmination of the band's frustration with journalists who tried to peg them as belonging to certain genres —"This ain't no glam rock, this ain't no K-Tel, this ain't no 'New Kid in Town'!"

Caterwauling puppets sprouted up all over the place in the late seventies, most notably in the state of Ohio — home to Pere Ubu, the Bizarros, Tin Huey, Woody Hayes, WKRP, King's Island amusement park, and the research and development wing of Union Carbide Industries, the latter of which operated with a precision and purity that would have been the envy of any Conehead band. As quirky and distinct from one another as they all were, the only Ohio band/unit/ division to come out lasers a-blazing was Devo, a group of ex-potato farmers from Akron who strongly believed that because humankind was spiralling backwards ('devolving') at a startling rate anyway, their own presence wasn't going to be too harmful one way or the other. Their famous debut album, *Q: Are We Not Men? A: We Are Devo!* (1978), generated a great deal of interest in the band's robot-stiff version of "(I Can't Get No) Satisfaction," which was rather unfair seeing as the Rolling Stones had put out an entire double-live album of robot-stiff cover versions a year earlier and all everyone did was complain. Like all Conehead bands, Devo had a strict policy against drugs, alcohol, smoking, junk food, and every other standard-fare rock-star vice; when they took to wearing flowerpots on their heads, however, they did have to be watered twice a week.

Coneheads also turned up on the beaches of Atlanta, where the B-52's depicted life as a giant frat party with baked potatoes for everyone. "Rock Lobster," the single from *The B-52's* (1979), sparked a national breakdancing craze during its "Down! Down!" section, but the album's best song was "52 Girls," which for the next couple years had people all over the world naming new baby girls either Madge, Hazel, or Mavis. Special mention must also be made of La Verne, creator of spectacular bouffants for B-52's Cindy and Kate; except for Don Cornelius, no one's hair was bigger in the seventies.

Meanwhile, a restless generation of Coneheads had begun to assert itself across the U.K. It was made up of young men and women who had been inspired by the likes of Johnny Moped and the Pork Dukes to form punk bands in 1977, but they now found themselves harkening back to the Sparks and Mike Oldfield records that captured their imaginations as teenagers. M's "Pop Muzik" (1979)[1] became the third new wave record to hit number one in America, and by virtue of the group's name it joined Al Stewart's "Year of the Cat," Alan Parsons' "The Raven," and Casablanca Records in the underappreciated seventies genre of Peter Lorre Rock. "Video Killed the Radio Star" by the Buggles entered *Billboard*'s Top 100 just as "Pop Muzik" started to drop, a week that also saw the chart debut of Sugarhill Gang's "Rapper's Delight"— a thrilling prophecy of the decade ahead for some but an alarming development in human bewilderment for HRS faithful.

Gary Numan took Conehead wave to a new plateau of aliena-tion, introspection, and unsolvable philosophical conundrum with "Are Friends Electric?" (1979), but on "Cars" (1979) he simply advised listeners "don't let the sound of your own wheels drive you crazy" and left it at that. XTC's "Life Begins at the Hop," the highlight of their *Drums and Wires* album (1979), had a teenage exuberance too often missing from Conehead wave, traceable perhaps to the days when leader Andy Partridge shook maracas behind Keith, Laurie, and Danny — Andy was their upper-class British cousin who every now and again paid a visit to the Partridge abode. The last word in this strange odyssey belongs to Ultravox, whose colorful titles were a map of the Conehead heart: "I Want To Be a Machine" (1977), "Hiroshima Mon Amour" (1977), *Systems of Romance* (1978), "A Circuit Torn Asun-der" (1978), and *Pale Mercurochrome Eyes* (1979) all exuded a

---

[1.] Actually the work of one guy, Robin Scott, with 'M' being short for 'Me'.

crystalline passion and four-function memory that are enchanting as ever some fifteen years later.

The first era of new wave climaxed with the release of the Fabulous Poodles' *Think Pink* in 1979. Here at last was a group that united the parallel but distinct worlds of Eraserheads and Coneheads, a group that did for these warring factions what Marion Keisker had once credited Elvis as doing for the whole of American popular music — the Poodles performed the "giant wedding ceremony," a key development in pop history that marked the beginning of Chowderhead wave. From that moment forward, new wave continued to mutate into ever newer and ever more intricate hairdos, until at some point in the early eighties it was decided that television ought to be there to document what was happening. This is where Kajagoogoo says hi and we say bye.

Chapter 29

ESCAPE (THE PINA COLADA CHAPTER)

"I saw Rick Wakeman playing in the States — terrific. He was
pushing a mellotron over an ice rink on skates trying to catch it.
That's art."
— Rick Neilsen, 1979.

AND that's it, fellow travellers, time to close the book on these,
the best years of our lives. In saying goodbye to the 1970s, there's
nobody better equipped to deliver the eulogy than Cheap Trick, the
premier bubblepunk/power-pop/disco-metal/new-wave/Ronco-trash/
hype-machine crazies of the decade. Not only that, one of us once
stood a stone's throw across a lake from guitarist Rick Neilsen's house
in Rockford, Illinois, placing us practically in the band's inner circle of
friends and associates.

The Cheap Trick story began in the early 1960s, when local thugs
Rick Neilsen and Tom Petersson were busy doing the "Louie Louie"
thing with various high school bands in the Great American Midwest.
It's important to remember these formative years when tracing Cheap
Trick's evolution, because time literally stopped for Rick and Tom in
a couple of ways: one, the arrival of the Beatles on U.S. shores had a
lasting influence on everything Cheap Trick would eventually record;
and two, Rick was so in love with his period costume of beanie, bow

tie, and varsity sweater (not even Gilbert O'Sullivan looked as collegiate as Ricky), he never again bought new clothes.

It wasn't until 1968 that Rick and Tom finally got an album out as part of the band Fuse; when the LP failed to sell the forty-five copies needed to break even, Fuse defused pronto. The next few years saw Rick and Tom hop back and forth between the United States and Europe, trying to get a band together that would build upon the Fuse legend. In Germany Bun E. Carlos, a seedy-looking character who used to pound horsehide in Sha Na Na-type revival shows, entered the picture. It was a touching and historic meeting: Bun E. took one look at Rick, Rick took one look at Bun E., and they both suddenly felt a whole lot better about themselves. Giddy with excitement, the three men waved down the first cab they saw marked 'Airport,' made the driver turn back when they realized they still needed a singer, picked up Robin Zander (another American expatriate) along the roadside, and, in 1974, set out for a triumphant homecoming.

It's a long, long way to Budokan, though, so for the next couple years the newly christened Cheap Trick traipsed around the U.S.A. playing upwards of 250 shows a year. Curious souls who ventured out for a look-see must not have known what to make of the band: too chirpy to be metal, too self-deprecating to be arty, too fast to 'lude-out to, too mischievous to trust, too quintessentially seventies to give a second thought to. Making matters even more confusing was the ascension of punk and disco in the mid-seventies, which, when combined with the proliferation of Ronco junk on Top Forty airwaves, created a climate that left shell-shocked pop fans without any emotional compass whatsoever. The time was exactly right for a group of semi-lovable nerf-munchkins to step forward and make sense of it all. If Dr. Hook or the Wombles couldn't do it, then maybe, just maybe, Cheap Trick could.

Cheap Trick, their first LP released early in 1977, was a good start in that direction. There were musical jokes and puns all over the place, snappy paeans to mass murder, paedophilia, suicide, and other popular American hobbies, and best of all there was "He's a Whore," the most gleefully malevolent we're-only-in-it-for-the-money confession of a decade with no shortage of them. "He's a Whore" was enough to land Cheap Trick an opening spot on the next Kiss tour: Paul

Stanley and Gene Simmons were so dismayed by such blatantly mercenary sentiments, they offered to take the upstart band under their wing and teach them the finer, more thoughtful path to rock and roll enlightenment.

Cheap Trick took their momentum from the Kiss tour and pumped it into *In Color*, their second LP released later that year. Clearly, here was a schizophrenic band for a schizophrenic time, one that had absorbed and mastered every stray chunk of refuse off the seventies scrapheap: traces of the Move, Todd Rundgren, the Raspberries, early Sweet, middle-period Partridge Family, side one of K-Tel's *20 Dynamite Hits!*, certain Uriah Heep albums of ill repute, anything and everything with melody and guitars and the overwhelming stamp of abject insignificance. The LP was highlighted by "I Want You To Want Me," which combined the unstoppable surge of First Class's "Beach Baby," the hardcore wussiness of Climax's "Precious and Few," and a swelling crescendo of "deedle-i-deedle-i-deedle-i"s. "Downed," "Southern Girls," and "Come On, Come On" were pretty fabulous too, while "Hello There" tossed out a metaphysical challenge that would henceforth jumpstart every Cheap Trick concert: "Hello there, ladies and gentlemen/Are you ready to rock?" The question was repeated about thirty-nine times, just so you had plenty of time to think up an answer.

Meanwhile, Cheap Trick's unique visual presentation was winning new converts daily. Robin and Tom blew kisses to the Andy Gibb/ *Tiger Beat* set, Bun E. perennially looked as if he'd just snuck out of a porno theatre, and Rick careened around concert stages like a crazed Pee Wee Herman forerunner. In 1978, the band released *Heaven Tonight*, a mixed collection that was kicked off by "Surrender," the first Cheap Trick single to chart (#62 — Bee Gees, here we come). It is here that we finally reach the end of the seventies rainbow, complete our journey downstream to capture Mr. Kurtz, draw the curtain on the Wizard once and for all, bow our heads humbly to the decade's Holy Grail, unlock the meaning of existence...we're running out of ill-advised metaphors, but you get the idea. "Surrender" was nothing less than miraculous: a mixed-up generational dialogue at once mysterious, celebratory, funny, humane, kinetic, roaring, able to say something profound without in any way trying to be profound, full of wisdom, affection, incredulity, and acceptance. It travelled from an army base in the Philippines to a living room in Illinois, where it ended with a single image that encapsulated a time, a place, and an entire wacked-out generation: a typical seventies glitter kid wakes up one night to find his parents orgying merrily to the romantic strains of his Kiss records. What was one supposed to do when confronted by such madness? Surrender, obviously — being a pop fan in the 1970s was a sustained act of day-by-day, year-by-year, outrage-by-outrage, gimmick-by-gimmick, improbability-by-improbability surrender. It was a lost-cause war of attrition, and ultimately it led to a fan's acceptance that even though the music could be as transporting as ever — "Surrender" was proof of that, not to mention "Rock and Roll All Nite," "I Feel Love," "Yo-Yo," "Get Down Tonight," and a hundred other unfathomable seventies masterpieces — only a lunatic could still believe that pop music's best days were ahead, the way one might have as the decade began. And that's where Cheap Trick's affection came in to elevate "Surrender" way beyond cynicism: keep something back for yourself anyway, it advised, because one day we'll look back and discover we were all right. Maybe we'll even feel nostalgic for the whole silly mess.

"Surrender" marked Cheap Trick as the truest of all seventies heroes, but in order to make it official they still had to attend to two things: 1) release a live album, and 2) become totally irrelevant by 1980. First up was *Cheap Trick at Budokan* (1979), which transformed one nation's worship into forty minutes of bang-up Godzilla ambience: lots of crash-boom-whomp, 20,000 Japanese teenagers screaming for mercy, an ungodly looking creature surveying the scene from above (Rick or Bun E., take your pick), and a nifty soundtrack to heighten the tension (made up of old favorites, a good new song called "Look Out," and a great version of "Surrender"). *Budokan* was still high on the charts when *Dream Police* (1979) came out, an album with all the signs of a band whose moment had passed. The title song was vintage Cheap Trick, but most of the rest was either ho-hum tired or outright inept, and the group was more or less a dead fish from that day forward. Tom left in 1980, and though the others carried on and rallied for a couple of late eighties hits, it was difficult to reconcile the new Cheap Trick with the one responsible for "He's a Whore," "Hello

There," "Surrender," and the rest. All that really remained from the glory days was Rick's uncanny influence as an arbiter of fashion, as teenagers everywhere began wearing baseball caps marked with the letter X (Rick's favorite algebraic symbol) in the early nineties. Can bow ties be far behind?

Goodnight now, ladies and gentlemen. That's the end of the show. Now it's time to go.

These are not 'the best' singles of the 1970s, they're our favorites. We compiled the list by picking fifty each and then filling in whatever gaps were created by overlap (ten songs were duplicated, and there were another half-dozen instances where we had different songs by the same artist). We limited ourselves to singles, which in almost all cases wasn't a limitation at all — it does explain, however, why the Rolling Stones aren't here, as none of their singles was as good as album tracks from *Sticky Fingers* and *Exile on Main St.* Chart rankings are American, though a few of the records with no ranking (e.g., "Heroes" and "Hong Kong Garden") did chart in Britain. To lead off, a couple of last-minute sixties releases that peaked just as the new decade got underway...

1. B.J. Thomas — "Raindrops Keep Fallin' On My Head" (11/69, #1)
2. Led Zeppelin — "Whole Lotta Love" (11/69, #4)
3. Chairmen of the Board — "Give Me Just a Little More Time" (1/70, #3)
4. Edison Lighthouse — "Love Grows (Where My Rosemary Goes)" (2/70, #5)
5. John Lennon — "Instant Karma (We All Shine On)" (2/70, #3)
6. Toots & the Maytals — "Pressure Drop" (3/70)
7. Vanity Fare — "Hitchin' a Ride" (3/70, #5)
8. Five Stairsteps — "O-o-h Child" (3/70, #8)
9. George Baker Selection — "Little Green Bag" (3/70, #21)
10. Freda Payne — "Band of Gold" (4/70, #3)
11. Alive & Kicking — "Tighter, Tighter" (6/70, #7)
12. Bobby Sherman — "Julie, Do Ya Love Me" (8/70, #5)
13. Jefferson Airplane — "Mexico" (9/70)
14. James Taylor — "Fire and Rain" (9/70, #3)
15. Jackson 5 — "I'll Be There" (9/70, #1)
16. Partridge Family — "I Think I Love You" (10/70, #1)
17. 5th Dimension — "One Less Bell To Answer" (10/70, #2)
18. Neil Young — "Only Love Can Break Your Heart" (10/70, #33)
19. Black Sabbath — "Paranoid" (11/70, #61)
20. Gordon Lightfoot — "If You Could Read My Mind" (12/70, #5)

21. Alice Cooper — "Eighteen" (2/71, #21)
22. Tommy James — "Draggin' the Line" (6/71, #4)
23. Undisputed Truth — "Smiling Faces Sometimes" (6/71, #3)
24. Stevie Wonder — "If You Really Love Me" (8/71, #8)
25. Guess Who — "Rain Dance" (8/71, #19)
26. Persuaders — "Thin Line Between Love & Hate" (8/71, #15)
27. Joni Mitchell — "Carey" (9/71, #93)
28. Carpenters — "Superstar" (9/71, #2)
29. Osmonds — "Yo-Yo" (9/71, #3)
30. Sly & the Family Stone — "Family Affair" (11/71, #1)
31. Carly Simon — "Anticipation" (12/71, #13)
32. Yes — "Roundabout" (2/72, #13)
33. Roberta Flack — "The First Time Ever I Saw Your Face" (3/72, #1)
34. Jackson Browne — "Doctor My Eyes" (3/72, #8)
35. Elton John — "Rocket Man" (5/72, #6)
36. T. Rex — "Metal Guru" (5/72)
37. Al Green — "I'm Still In Love With You" (7/72, #3)
38. Rod Stewart — "You Wear It Well" (8/72, #13)
39. Mott the Hoople — "All the Young Dudes" (9/72, #37)
40. War — "The World Is a Ghetto" (11/72, #7)
41. Slade — "Gudbuy T' Jane" (3/73, #68)
42. Steely Dan — "Reeling In the Years" (3/73, #11)
43. Bob Dylan — "Knockin' on Heaven's Door" (9/73, #12)
44. Ringo Starr — "Photograph" (10/73, #1)
45. Todd Rundgren — "Hello It's Me" (10/73, #5)
46. New York Dolls — "Trash" (11/73)
47. Stylistics — "You Make Me Feel Brand New" (3/74, #2)
48. George McCrae — "Rock Your Baby" (6/74, #1)
49. Dionne Warwick & the Spinners — "Then Came You" (7/74, #1)
50. Carl Douglas — "Kung Fu Fighting" (10/74, #1)
51. Gloria Gaynor — "Never Can Say Goodbye" (11/74, #9)
52. Harold Melvin & the Blue Notes — "Bad Luck" (3/75, #15)
53. Melissa Manchester — "Midnight Blue" (5/75, #6)
54. Bachman-Turner Overdrive — "Hey You" (5/75, #21)
55. Aerosmith — "Sweet Emotion" (6/75, #36)
56. ABBA — "SOS" (8/75, #15)

57. Modern Lovers — "Roadrunner" (9/75)
58. April Wine — "Tonite Is a Wonderful Time To Fall in Love" (10/75)
59. O'Jays — "I Love Music" (11/75, #5)
60. Sweet — "Fox on the Run" (11/75, #5)
61. Kiss — "Rock and Roll All Nite" (live version) (11/75, #12)
62. Patti Smith — "Gloria" (2/76)
63. Maxine Nightingale — "Right Back Where We Started From" (2/76, #2)
64. Diana Ross — "Love Hangover" (4/76, #1)
65. Bay City Rollers — "Rock and Roll Love Letter" (5/76, #28)
66. Vicki Sue Robinson — "Turn the Beat Around" (4/76, #10)
67. Blue Oyster Cult — "(Don't Fear) the Reaper" (7/76, #12)
68. Nick Lowe — "So It Goes" (8/76)
69. Boston — "More Than a Feeling" (9/76, #5)
70. Sex Pistols — "Anarchy in the U.K." (12/76)
71. Fleetwood Mac — "Go Your Own Way" (1/77, #10)
72. Germs — "Forming" (6/77)
73. Ramones — "Sheena Is a Punk Rocker" (7/77, #81)
74. KC & the Sunshine Band — " Keep It Comin' Love" (7/77, #2)
75. Donna Summer — "I Feel Love" (8/77, #6)
76. Adverts — "Gary Gilmore's Eyes" (8/77)
77. Dolly Parton — "Here You Come Again" (10/77, #3)
78. David Bowie — "Heroes" (10/77)
79. Tavares — "More Than a Woman" (11/77, #32)
80. Bee Gees — "Night Fever" (2/78, #1)
81. Warren Zevon — "Werewolves of London" (3/78, #21)
82. X-Ray Spex — "The Day the World Turned Dayglo" (4/78)
83. Walter Egan — "Magnet and Steel" (5/78, #8)
84. Taste of Honey — "Boogie Oogie Oogie" (6/78, #1)
85. Exile — "Kiss You All Over" (7/78, #1)
86. Cheap Trick — "Surrender" (7/78, #62)
87. Siouxsie & the Banshees — "Hong Kong Garden" (8/78)
88. Stiff Little Fingers — "Alternative Ulster" (8/78)
89. Avengers — "The Amerikan in Me" (10/78)
90. Sylvester — "You Make Me Feel (Mighty Real)" (1/79, #36)
91. Peaches & Herb — "Reunited" (3/79, #1)

92. Van Halen — "Dance the Night Away" (4/79, #15)
93. McFadden & Whitehead — "Ain't No Stoppin' Us Now" (4/79, #13)
94. Raydio — "You Can't Change That" (4/79, #9)
95. XTC — "Life Begins at the Hop" (5/79)
96. Anita Ward — "Ring My Bell" (5/79, #1)
97. Chic — "Good Times" (6/79, #1)
98. Patrick Hernandez — "Born To Be Alive" (8/79, #16)
99. Michael Jackson — "Don't Stop 'Til You Get Enough" (7/79, #1)
100. Police — "Message in a Bottle" (11/79, # 74)

About the Authors

Phil Dellio lives in Georgetown, Ontario, where he works as a supply teacher for the Peel Board of Education. He has written for *Nerve!*, *Graffiti*, *Innings*, and *Radio On*.

Scott Woods lives in Toronto and has written for *Radio On*, *Nerve!*, *Graffiti*, and *Rock Box*.

Dave Prothero lives in Toronto and works as a freelance illustrator.

I Wanna Be Sedated
Pop Music in the Seventies

First published in Canada by

Sound And Vision
359 Riverdale Avenue
Toronto, Canada M4J 1A4

First printing; September 1993.
15.13.11.9.7.5.3.1. -printings- 2.4.6.8.10.12.14
99.97.95.93. -year- 94.96.98.

Canadian Cataloguing in Publication Data

Dellio, Phil, 1961-
I wanna be sedated : pop music in the seventies

ISBN 0-920151-16-7

1. Popular music —1971-1980-Humor. 2. Rock music - 1971 - Humor. 3. Satire, Canadian (English) - 20th century. I. Woods, Scott, 1964- II. Title.

ML3470.D45 1993   782.42164   C93-094980-3

Printed and bound in Canada on acid free paper